Understanding and Loving Your Child as a Single Parent

UNDERSTANDING AND LOVING YOUR CHILD

AS A SINGLE PARENT

STEPHEN ARTERBURN
and **STACEY SADLER**

SALEM
BOOKS
an imprint of Regnery Publishing
Washington, D.C.

Scripture quotations marked BBE are taken from the 1949/1964 BIBLE IN BASIC ENGLISH, public domain.

Scripture quotations marked KJV are taken from the King James Version, public domain.

Scripture quotations marked MSG are taken from THE MESSAGE. Copyright © 1993, 1994, 1995, 1996, 2000, 2001, 2002. Used by permission of NavPress Publishing Group.

Scripture quotations marked NIV are taken from the Holy Bible, New International Version®, NIV®. Copyright © 1973, 1978, 1984, 2011 by Biblica, Inc. ® Used by permission of Zondervan. All rights reserved worldwide. www.zondervan.com. The "NIV" and "New International Version" are trademarks registered in the United States Patent and Trademark Office by Biblica, Inc.®

Scriptures marked NLT are taken from the Holy Bible, New Living Translation. Copyright © 1996, 2004, 2015 by Tyndale House Foundation. Used by permission of Tyndale House Ministries, Carol Stream, Illinois 60188. All rights reserved.

Scripture quotations marked RSV are taken from the Revised Standard Version of the Bible. Copyright © 1946, 1952, and 1971 National Council of the Churches of Christ in the United States of America. Used by permission. All rights reserved.

Salem Books™ is a trademark of Salem Communications Holding Corporation. Regnery® is a registered trademark and its colophon is a trademark of Salem Communications Holding Corporation.

Cataloging-in-Publication data on file with the Library of Congress

ISBN: 978-1-68451-155-6
eISBN: 978-1-68451-318-5

Library of Congress Control Number: 2022938952

Published in the United States by
Salem Books
An Imprint of Regnery Publishing
A Division of Salem Media Group
Washington, D.C.
www.SalemBooks.com

Manufactured in the United States of America

10 9 8 7 6 5 4 3 2 1

Books are available in quantity for promotional or premium use. For information on discounts and terms, please visit our website: www.SalemBooks.com.

For Zach and Whitney. I love you with all my heart

To my mom and dad in Heaven, who both left a rich legacy of touching people's lives

To all the courageous single parents persevering every day to be excellent

To my tribe of encouraging friends and family for keeping me going

To God, who makes all things possible

CONTENTS

Introduction

Perhaps, like me, you did not choose to be a single parent. That was pushed on me when my previous wife divorced me and I became the primary parent of my daughter, Madeline. We become single parents due to death, defiance, drift, or divorce. More important than how we got here, however, is what we do when faced with such a difficult challenge. It is easy to sink down into despair, not realizing how far we have fallen. It takes courage (and humble willingness to adjust and adapt) in order to rise up and meet the challenges of being a competent single parent.

It turns out that being a single parent to Madeline was one of the greatest joys of my life. It was not because I knew everything and Madeline responded like a perfectly predictable robot. She had a mind of her own, and the choices she made were most often good ones. (Perhaps my gift to her was not to mess things up beyond repair.) Through it all, I had some very good mentors, coaches, and encouragers, like Dr. Henry Cloud, Dr. John Townsend, and Dr. Jill Hubbard. Their wisdom is reflected in this book. I did not know Stacey Sadler back then, but she would have been a great help if I had.

For many years, Stacey has been one of New Life's most valued facilitators at our weekend intensive workshops. She is trained as a clinician, but she is especially effective in treating trauma and the impact of betrayal on the partners of sex addicts. She is so knowledgeable and effective that I asked her to serve on the board of directors.

Stacey has put all of her wisdom and knowledge to work as a single parent in her own life. Her adult children are a tribute to her single parenting in the toughest of times. She is an excellent communicator, and I believe you will find her writing meaningful and easily applicable to your situation. The writing is mostly in her voice, but you will see contributions from me throughout the book as well.

Stephen Arterburn
March 2022

CHAPTER 1

You Got This: Parenting Well

Being a single parent is twice the work, twice the stress, and twice the tears, but also twice the hugs, twice the love, and twice the pride.

Unknown

"I can't do this alone!" I said as I bemoaned my fate to my two dear friends. As we sat at my breakfast room table, all my dams of composure and self-respect broke. My friends were seeing me at my pathetic worst. I couldn't hold back the reality of my situation, and my desperate feelings of rejection and betrayal came flowing out: I was going through a divorce and would be walking the road of a single parent.

"I feel so invisible and disregarded, like I am worth nothing," I said.

Luckily, God sent friends to walk this road with me. These moments were temporary, and thankfully, moments of victory followed. Somehow, I would manage to get it together, run a few miles, take an online class, pick a kid up from school, and help my children with homework. Then there were the really positive days that I remember exclaiming, "I am woman! Hear me roar!" There was the day I successfully fixed the leaky grease trap under my sink, and the time I fixed my oven door lock switch by myself. Tasks that previously had seemed beyond my abilities, YouTube made doable for me.

Every now and then, I'd slip back into self-pity. I struggled to accept my newly single status in a church I had belonged to for years. "I don't want to be here," I told my new single moms' Sunday school class. "I am supposed to be in the married class." Some of the members looked at me and said, "Newsflash, neither do we!" I was shortsighted to think that I was alone in my singleness. When I grasped that fact, I was able to embrace a reality that I did not want, and I began to take steps to change what I could.

Yes, being a single parent is challenging. The days can be long. It may feel like there is not enough of you to go around. Financial stressors can add to the strain of being the only decision maker. There may be less quality time with each child when no other parent will pick up the slack. Often, single parents feel like they have no time for themselves, because even when the kids are out of the house, they can be too tired to do anything but sleep.

When you parent alone, discipline falls squarely on your shoulders; no one else can play "bad cop." If any family members experience a sense of loss, stress can permeate the entire household. You could be living with your parents, or at a lower economic standard than what you had envisioned for yourself. Maybe you have been forced to live in an unsafe area. These are all common scenarios for single parents.

Newsworthy Single-Parent Homes

Being raised in a non-traditional home need not be a recipe for maladjustment. Many folks—public figures and ordinary people alike—attribute their success to the values they learned from their single parents. Here's how a Georgia mom is making the best of her circumstances: "While I cannot be both a mother and father, I can teach my teen daughters about Jesus and be an example of a godly woman," she explained in a Focus on the Family online article. "I'll never be the perfect parent, but I can lead our family in becoming more Christ-like."[1]

On the celebrity front, TV news anchor Katie Couric is doing all she can do to turn pain into promise for her kids. Her children were two and six years old when her husband succumbed to colon cancer, but she continued to raise them while flourishing in her career as a *CBS Evening News* anchor. Other notable celebrities, like Olympic swimmer Michael Phelps, NBA legend Shaquille O'Neal, and movie star Samuel L. Jackson, were raised by single parents and found success despite the challenges they faced at home. Political news satirist Stephen Colbert's mother raised him alone after his father and two brothers were killed in a plane crash. Many children of single parents say they developed a deep bond with their parent that propelled them toward their dreams. Watching their single parent work hard and sacrifice can create a sense of gratitude in children.[2]

Perks of Obligation

While many single parents don't have the luxury of spoiling their children, the necessity of their circumstance can actually help create a good work ethic. Kids who help run the household benefit in several ways, including collaborating with coworkers, fostering independent work habits, and developing compassion for others.[3] Children who help with chores develop a good work ethic and a sense of teamwork. Children who have fostered independence and responsibility at a young age have greater self-esteem.[4] On the flipside, children in both single- and two-parent homes can become entitled and lazy if they get everything they want and are not expected to work for it. This, according to one psychotherapist, appears to be a problem of epidemic proportions these days.[5] "Many factors in modern parenting contribute to the crisis in kids' work ethics," writes Victoria Prooday, the founder and clinical director of a multi-disciplinary clinic for children and parents. "As parents, we bubble-wrap our kids and keep them in their comfort zone."[6] These kids may struggle as they enter the workforce later in life.

Your kids may complain and blame you, but trust me, they benefit from helping with the running of the household, whether they know it or not. Another perk of obligation is the appreciation that our children develop for what they do have. When he was in his teens, my son, Zach, chose to work at Sherwin-Williams to get spending money. The next summer, he worked for an air-conditioning company to earn extra funds to buy a nicer car. Today, Zach appreciates the nice, cool office where he works as an engineer. He says, "I knew I never wanted to work in a hot attic again! So, I worked hard to make the grades to land a white-collar job."

Another dividend of having household chores out of neces-sity is accountability. There were many days that my two kids and I felt like a team; none of us wanted to rock the boat of our lives that had finally become stable. We held each other accountable to work hard and do our part to make our "new normal" run smoothly.

And for the single parent? Though you do have to shoulder all the parenting weight alone, you also have complete control over the culture of your home. Parental conflict has been found to lower academic achievement and increase substance use in children.[7] When only one parent is in the home, children are exposed less often to active disagreements. The power in your hands to teach healthy communication and model healthy social skills has a positive effect on maturing offspring. My family experienced this. I was able to discuss the bottom line with them and had no one to refute it. The buck stopped with me, and my kids knew it. I had control over the type of movies they were watching, whom they dated, and what consequences they would face when they disobeyed.

When I found out some of their friends weren't allowed to use cell phones at mealtimes, I followed suit. To compensate, I put a pack of conversation-starter cards next to the salt and pepper shakers, filled with questions like, "If you could wake up every morning, open your bedroom blinds, and look out a huge glass window at the perfect view, what would that view be?" So, when my kids got bored at the table, their little fingers inevitably ended up pulling one out. Not only did this help me and my kids get to know and respect each other on a deeper level, it also developed the conversational skills they would need in life, which electronics inhibit.

God Cares for Single Parents

Did you know there are single moms in the Bible? Hagar, the slave girl, laid with Abraham at the request of her mistress, Sarah—but after Hagar gave birth to Ishmael, Sarah banished her into the wilderness. As she sat, despairing in the desert in fear that her son would die of dehydration, God saw Hagar and recognized her struggle. We read in Genesis 21:17–20 that an angel of God appeared to her and said,

> What is the matter, Hagar? Do not be afraid; God has heard the boy crying as he lies there. Lift the boy up and take him by the hand, for I will make him into a great nation.

Then, God opened Hagar's eyes and she saw a well of water, so she filled a skin with water and gave Ishmael a drink. God was with the boy as he grew up. God thinks highly of single parents. He uses any means necessary to provide for us!

Even though you might feel invisible or like a second-class citizen, God thinks you are pretty special. Open your eyes and see what He is showing you, listen to what He is whispering to you, and open your heart to believe that He will partner with you.

Many others have walked the path that you are walking. I will introduce you to them—their struggles, their mistakes, their successes, and their rewards—in the pages of this book. You will identify with their pain, laugh with their missteps, and cheer for their wins. As you become equipped, your children will learn that difficult circumstances don't have to define your family. They will watch you overcome, day after day. They will see you make mistakes, apologize, ask for a do-over, and then do better. They will learn to be resilient. They will learn how to thrive in life as they watch you thrive.

CHAPTER 2

In the Beginning: Surviving the Early Days

I have been driven many times upon my knees by the overwhelming conviction that I had nowhere else to go. My own wisdom and that of all about me seemed insufficient for that day.

Abraham Lincoln

Loella blindly stumbled down the hallway to my office. In a completely befuddled state, she began to talk about how to "play nice" with her estranged spouse, from whom she was separated. For Loella, "playing nice" meant walking on eggshells to avoid igniting the powder keg of her husband's anger. She was trying to decide how to talk to her kids about the separation in a truthful way that wouldn't set her husband off if it got back to him. She reluctantly agreed to tell them that he was away on business. For the past month, she had been admitting the truth about her husband to herself. She was grappling with her idealized version of her life and what was actually happening.

"He really is my best friend . . ." Loella told me, her voice quavering. She needed to plan a graduation party for her daughter, whose anxiety made it hard for her to even think about crossing the stage. Loella admitted, "I'm scared I am going to do it wrong." Several weeks went by like this, as she tried to hold all the pieces together as they were quickly falling apart. It got to be too much, and she finally filed for divorce because she couldn't stand her husband's blatant infidelity—especially the fact that he was being unfaithful to her with much younger *men.*

"I'm afraid and it's not okay," she told me. "I taught myself not to feel fear, but in the process I made myself a victim."

Loella had been thinking that if she just played her part as the dutiful wife and mother, she could make it all okay.

It's Not So Easy at Times

Sometimes, we carry way too much. Somehow, we grow up believing the old adage, "Don't worry about the horse, just load the wagon." We believe we get a gold medal for not having limitations. But the words that no self-respecting perfectionist would ever say—"I can't handle it"—are actually very freeing. Eventually, you do have to worry about the horse. You have to check in with yourself and ask, "How am I truly functioning?" Are you on autopilot, like Loella? Are you too keyed up to sleep? Can you admit that you need some help? Look further into the future. Can you sustain your current pace for the long haul?

When you first realize you are going to be a single parent, you likely enter survival mode, which means you conserve your resources. This means you take an honest inventory of what is sucking your energy away, and you scale those things back. You may be plagued with negative self-talk as you curtail your activities. Listen to what you are saying to yourself when you decline invitations! You might be surprised to find a critical voice commenting on your limited abilities. Usually, the word "should" pervades these thoughts. Listen and become aware, then record the most negative comments in a journal. You might be surprised to find a committee in your head that has condemned you as worthless. You wouldn't talk to your best friend that way (at least, I hope not), so why would you talk to yourself that way? After documenting these thoughts, begin trying to stop them.

While you cut back, you have to be kind to yourself and send messages of care and kindness to your inner being. Think about how good you feel when someone offers you compassion and understanding. These reassurances create a sense of safety and stabilization in your body, brain, and spirit. Do that for yourself always, but especially in your early days as a single parent.

The ANTeater in Your Brain

Dr. Daniel Amen, a psychiatrist and brain disorder specialist, studies brains all day, every day. He uses SPECT (single-photon emission computed tomography) scans to map the brain to see how it responds to different stimuli. He notes the interconnected physiological effects of thinking patterns on the brain and body. Dr. Amen says that when we have negative, judgmental thoughts that he calls ANTs (Automatic Negative Thoughts), our brains release chemicals that make our bodies feel distressed. Symptoms include rapid heartbeat, muscle tension, and faster breathing. Memory, judgment, and logical reasoning decrease. When we send ourselves positive, hopeful messages, our bodies respond by becoming more relaxed. Our breathing slows, our muscles relax, and our brains are able to work more efficiently. Dr. Amen suggests employing an "ANTeater to patrol the streets of your mind."[1] For instance, if an ANT says, "I can't do this," you change it to "I *can* do this with the help of God and others." When you are facing new challenges, and an ANT screams, "You should know how to do things alone!" turn that around to "I can take steps to learn how to do something alone." (More about this in chapter 18.)

Faith Foundation

I have a painting hanging on the wall in my office. It is a very unassuming canvas, consisting of yellow and green horizontal stripes of graduating sizes. It looks a little like a sunset. I received it early in my practicum while working at a crisis pregnancy center. When a newly single parent is struggling with his or her own sense of weakness, I get up, grab the painting off the wall, and tell this story:

Lucia was a client, and she was really depressed. When I asked her what she had loved to do as a child, she told me that she loved painting. I asked if she was still painting. She told me no. She said that her husband told her they didn't have room in their tiny apartment for her painting materials. He also said that they couldn't afford to buy new canvases. I told her to find a corner, even if it was in the kitchen, and use old canvases, even if she had to paint over them. Just get painting again, I told her! She was an obedient client and took my suggestion. Her depression started to improve, and she began to find her lost heart. She began to have hope again.

In appreciation, Lucia painted this sunset for me. It graces the wall behind my clients as they sit on my couch. As I move across my office and reach over them to take the painting off the wall, I continue, "So, when I got my new office, I put this painting in the window, like this"—and I dramatically place it in the window.

As the sunlight comes through the back of the painting, a picture of Jesus appears. You really have to see it to believe it. My client's jaws predictably drop. I then say, "I called Lucia and asked how she did that magnificent thing. She had no idea what I was talking about, until I explained that there is a picture of Jesus behind the painting of the sunset that is virtually undetectable when on the wall. She told me that she followed my suggestion and painted over some pictures of Jesus that she didn't like."

Wow! My client and I usually just look for a minute at our Savior staring back at us. I then quote 2 Corinthians 4:7: "We now have this light shining in our hearts, but we ourselves are like fragile clay jars containing this great treasure. This makes it clear that our great power is from God, not from ourselves" (NLT). If, in your solo parenting, you are a tough piece of pottery, God's glory cannot show itself. But if you are fragile, limited, and have a few cracks, His richness can show up and show off most often on your behalf.

Superhero

Another client, Gena, fondly refers to herself as "Wonder Woman"—probably because she needs a constant reminder that she *can* do it. I think it is very possible that Gena's support system helped crown her with that title. When parenting on your own feels impossible without superpowers granted to us from on high, a superhero reference can be helpful. What single parent doesn't want Spidey senses, super speed, or a little shapeshifting in order to get everything done? But, while we occasionally need reminders of our super strength, we need to lay down the cape and let God be God.

Even Superman has his kryptonite. We know that he doesn't succumb long to the powerful radioactive poison. But it does force him to pause for a while, regroup, and develop another strategy. Often in single parenting, we must do the same. When struck down by the realities of mortal weakness, we have to accept our limitations and agree to receive help. Specifics of how to receive help will be covered in chapters 8 and 9. The bottom line is that Superman is still super even when he has been broken down by kryptonite. And Wonder Woman is still wonderful even when she can't use telepathy to understand what her kids *aren't* saying. Your value is not in your ability to perform. There is way more to you than that! Your worth is in the fact that the Savior of the Universe gave His life for you and would do it again, over and over, because He loves you that much.

Tools for Successful Resource Management

You have likely heard the expression "my plate is full." Take a minute to consider your plate of life. Each of your activities and commitments are items on your plate. Now, visualize emptying your plate. That's it, clean it off. Observe the clean plate. Now, add back each item in order of priority. Only replate what you can comfortably handle.

When emptying, ask yourself the following questions:

What can I scale back on?

Can I completely subtract this responsibility?

Can I release this obligation or delegate it to someone else?

When replating, ask yourself:

Is this life-giving?

Is it a top priority?

Is this really my responsibility, or someone else's?

What happens if I don't do this?

As you unload responsibilities, seek God for guidance. So often, we forget that we have the Holy Spirit residing in us to help us discern direction and priorities. Take time to notice what feelings arise as you scale back your commitments. Listed below are some of the common self-denigrating beliefs—Automatic Negative Thoughts—that can deplete a new single parent.

ANTs:

I should be able to do it all.

I am weak.

A good parent would . . .

I should have more energy.

I am not good enough.

I am a loser.

I can't ever do it right.

I am not as good as . . .

ANTeaters:

I am reserving my energy.

I need rest.

I am accepted by God.

I am a good parent.

I can't handle that.

It's okay to relax.

I am enough.

The Gift That Keeps On Giving

Be a good steward of your resources for your children. Model balance for them. Mimic God's design for a day of Sabbath. Your children will feel the effects of your balanced parenting by the vibe you give off. This "vibe" will give them permission to have limitations themselves. This is the best defense you can give them against performance-based living. They will see that it is okay to say no, okay to rest, and okay to admit that you have limits, beyond which your efforts become ineffective. They will learn to depend on God instead of merely their own resources. Who doesn't want to help develop this kind of faith in their children?

My daughter's friend Allie learned a valuable lesson from watching her dad take a week off during the holidays after his divorce. He knew he was grieving and couldn't do his best at work and at home. A month later, when Allie broke up with her boyfriend, she tearfully announced, "Dad, I think I need a mental health day from school today." Her dad obliged, and together, they learned that it is okay to have limits.

These are the steps to owning your limitations as a single parent:

First, become aware of them. Honestly assess your ability to manage your health and your responsibilities in this new stage. This is when you assess your plate to see if it is well balanced or overflowing.

Second, take steps to unload some obligations. This is when you empty your plate.

Then, when you are ready to reload your plate, ask those questions in the previous section to assess whether the activity or responsibility you are considering is life-giving. Set boundaries and reset your expectations for yourself. Become an ANTeater: battle the negative thoughts and change them into life-giving statements that will rebalance your psyche. Accepting that you are not always Superman or Wonder Woman does not discount who you are as a person. Become balanced in your being and model humility for your children.

You can do this! You are now aware that having limitations is normal. You know now that negative self-talk has deleterious effects on your body and brain. You have the tools to make your plate more manageable and be compassionate with yourself. Begin making these changes so that your children will see a stable parent handling life well. Now, let's learn ways to navigate the difficult feelings that accompany single parenthood.

CHAPTER 3

Mask On or Mask Off?: Feeling Your Grief

*Grief is not a disorder, a disease, or a sign of weakness.
It is an emotional, physical, and spiritual necessity, the
price you pay for love. The only cure for
grief is to grieve.*

Earl Grollman

I lost the beach in the divorce. There are so many losses that come with divorce. Crazy little things like the purple popcorn bowl that he must've hijacked, or the fingernail clippers that I regularly found in the same little manicure set in the bathroom drawer where it resided for twenty-four years. These little landmines exploded as I unknowingly stepped on them, and, shockingly, tears began spilling out of my eyes before I knew what was happening. Nothing, however, was as poignant as the loss of the beach.

I grew up fishing with my dad on Lake Conroe. Nothing beat putting a little Mighty Mealy worm on the end of the hook and pulling up perch after perch from the lake. The deck hand (my dad) removed each fish and rebaited me so I could do it over and over again. My excitement in catching a fish became infectious. I developed a love for the sport. When I met my husband and he introduced me to saltwater fishing, I was literally hooked!

As I walked the beach with my friends while separated, I reminisced over the times that my ex-husband and I night-fished on the Bolivar pier trying to catch the elusive flounder. As I walked with Telicia and Sherri, the pain was palpable.

"I have lost the beach . . . it will never be the same."

They gave me their full attention as I wept and we walked. I shared stories about times my husband and I had shared at the seaside. I felt like I could fill the ocean with my salty tears. They patiently listened as I eulogized those times and pronounced a death sentence on any future fishing. They empathized as I lamented the loss of our home on the brackish water of Caney Creek where we taught our kids to crab, fish, and throw endless cast nets. I ached over my loss of the beach as my painted toenails dug into the sand with each stride. Yet grief can keep us from seeing the beauty right in front of us. While my life was forever altered, the beach was still there. After all, there I was, walking on it with friends. The truth was, my pain had blinded me.

Stephen

The Work of Grief

Stacey's walk on the beach underscores a necessary part of her transition: grief. It's the single most important factor in healing, but it's a step most people avoid like the plague. This ultimately keeps them stuck. As a therapist, Stacey knew she had to let herself grieve and eventually get on with her life.

You likely have heard about the stages of grief. In her book *On Death and Dying*, released in the early 1970s, Elizabeth Kübler-Ross[1] defined denial, anger, depression, bargaining, and acceptance as the five stages one goes through while grieving. Although originally written as an account of what patients experienced while dying, this model can guide us through all kinds of losses. The important thing to remember is that these stages are not a sequenced guide in how to survive a loss. Grief is a chaotic, sloppy journey, full of bombshells and blues. If we don't allow ourselves to grieve, but instead suppress those feelings, we run the risk of burying the grief alive. If this happens, we can end up stuck and unable to move forward in life.

Maybe your grief is not about a divorce. It could be that you came into single parenting through death of your spouse, or maybe your spouse abandoned you and/or your child. Whether you choose to become a single parent or the choice was made for you, there are still losses associated with it that need to be grieved. Some of those losses include not having a helpmate or a nuclear family. But this is where things get tricky. At the beginning stages of single parenthood, we often drift into denial. Many individuals Stacey and I work with continue to act as if life hasn't changed, that the loss hasn't occurred. Usually, this rejection of reality causes problems as time goes on and it becomes impossible to ignore the actuality of the situation. Denial can be a curse, but it also can be a temporary blessing. We see denial as a protective measure given by God to help usher us gently into a new leg of our journey. Just make sure you are moving through it, not remaining stuck in it.

I tell people all the time that anger, fear, and sadness are all healthy, appropriate, and *valid* emotions, but we are not meant to hang out in them for an extended period of time. As we move into anger and sadness, those emotions are often either unacceptable to us or become overwhelming, so we go into the stage of bargaining. This is where most of us get stuck in "why me?" or "it's not fair." It's an easier place to be than the pain. The problem is that those questions never get answered, and the situation never becomes fair. We have to go back to process those uncomfortable feelings and resolve them so we can move to the final stage, acceptance. But if we can't get there on our own, it's time to get help from a professional or a support group.

A New Habit

The fear about feeling strong emotions is that they will never go away or they will be too difficult to tolerate. What we know about properly processed emotions is that they follow a bell curve from increasing intensity to peaking and then decreasing in magnitude. Many clients stop right before the peak and escape the emotion before it is fully felt and processed.

Spiritual bypass is a common escape behavior. It goes something like this: "I know God is good all the time, and I will get through this." While this is a true statement, many times we say it to avoid the uncomfortable feelings beneath the spirituality. In this way, spiritualizing is used to ignore pain and emotional turmoil. We believe you won't heal unless you feel the difficult feelings and process them, and *then* let the truth of God's word comfort you.

Another escape behavior is humor. Have you ever seen someone smiling or making a joke right as they are getting ready to tear up? It's a great way to avoid difficult emotions. The problem here is that a person feels the pain and believes that it will hurt too much, so he subconsciously develops a belief that he can't tolerate it, or that it will continue forever. Then, he moves away from the emotion. While this protective belief feels temporarily comforting, the pain persists, because it sits unprocessed in the part of the brain called the amygdala.[2]

In therapy, we gently nudge individuals a little further along the bell curve to the peak of their emotions. As they feel the peak and the emotion recedes, they gain a sense of relief and resolve. The old belief is unfrozen, and the clients begin feeling the full range of emotions. They begin to believe that they can tolerate difficult emotions. When they learn that the emotions will pass, they are able to let themselves feel and move past the pain. This habituation makes processing feelings the norm and escaping them a thing of the past.[3] Part of the practice of mindfulness is learning to tolerate difficult emotions. When we learn to permit uncomfortable feelings, they no longer master us, and we can resolve the disturbance within our mind, body, and spirit.

Stacey

Precious Tears

During a pivotal time in my healing process, I journeyed across the globe to Athens, Greece, to take a course for my master's degree in counseling. A peculiar jar caught my attention as I shopped one day. Made of terra cotta, it was long and slender, with a flat lip all the way around the top. The shopkeeper saw me studying the vessel and reached for it. A somber look washed over his face as he put it to his eye, pretending to cry. Ah, I thought, a tears jar. I later learned that it was called a lachrymatory. I knew that it would be the first thing to grace the shelves of my future counseling office. Lachrymatories were common in ancient Rome. Mourners used them, then placed them in burial tombs to signify love and respect for the dead.[4] As I was drawn to this piece, Psalm 56:8 flooded my mind: "You keep track of all my sorrows. You have collected all my tears in your bottle, You have recorded each other in your book" (NLT). The psalmist David mentions this conviction that God truly documents each incident of our sorrow, and He knows and understands our pain. Buying a lachrymatory seemed like a fitting way to validate grief in my life and in the lives of all I would counsel.

As we flip through the Psalms, we see the rawness of human emotion filling the pages. The psalmists articulate and legitimize emotion, as their prayers rhythmically flow between expression and alleviation of distress. As the psalmists declare negative feelings, they ameliorate symptoms of disturbance and begin to praise the Almighty. The Psalms create a symphony of affliction whirling about, which then shifts into tranquility. This pattern follows the bell curve we discussed earlier. It also provides a comforting hope for life's trials.

Tools

A friend and colleague of ours, Dr. Sheri Keffer, once had this to say about moving from grief and loss to acceptance: "You've gotta cry a river of tears and get angry before you can get from one side of the river shore—grief or loss—to the other side of the shore, acceptance."[5]

Sadness and anger are the two essential emotions to process while grieving. Most people tend to hang out in one over the other. Which emotion you feel will help determine what you need to do to heal. If you hang out in anger, it's probably a good idea to tap into those more vulnerable feelings of sadness and loss. You may reject this idea because anger has become a comfortable place to live. It is protective, powerful, and keeps further hurt at a distance.

Journaling is a great way to start your process. Stick with it, even if it is uncomfortable. Whether your loss was a day ago or a decade ago, here are a few prompts to start you on your way.

What I miss most is . . .

What I wish above all is that . . .

What makes me angry is . . .

What breaks my heart the most is . . .

My biggest regret is . . .

On the other hand, you may set your campsite on the riverside of tears and melancholy. If this is you, the swim across the brook to anger is extremely uncomfortable. However, it is what you need to access to heal fully. Old ideas about any variety of anger being a sin can keep you from moving forward. Many therapists recommend directing your anger in a letter to those that have hurt you. These letters are a form of journaling meant to stimulate the healing process and are never meant to be received by the violator. However, something physical to release the stored-up tension in your body is really curative. Here's a list of ideas:

- Take a hammer to ice cubes and bust away.
- Write your grievance on eggs and throw them against a tree.
- Write your objection on golf balls and whack the heck out of them.
- Trim trees while reciting your protest.
- Whack an object against a bed or a pillow and let your outrage flow.

I had twenty-four years of memories to sift through as I prepared to leave the house my husband and I had shared. One of the dozens of boxes surrounding me was for breakable trash: vases, plates, and jars that weren't moving on with me. When the large trash dumpster arrived, I proceeded to hurl these fragile little things against its metal walls. I was invigorated by the purgative practice of physically stating my objection to my new reality. I discovered that baby food jars are virtually undestroyable. Thus, it took the nitrous full-throttle switch to finally explode those little jewels into a thousand pieces. So. Very. Satisfying. I then collapsed in tears from the sheer exhaustion of allowing what had been pent up for so many years to surface. This process was so cathartic. I do recommend breaking things (in a safe manner, of course!).

Teaching Appropriate Affect

Every day, we hear parents not expressing emotions around their children because they want to protect them. Actually, the very opposite happens. When parents shield their kids from appropriate emotions, they send a message that is inconsistent with the situation at hand. For instance, going through a breakup should be sad. If the parent does not allow the child to see his sadness, the child begins to believe that the sadness she herself is feeling must be wrong. This confuses children. When someone dies, we grieve, we cry. When there is an injustice, we get angry. When someone betrays us we are shocked, then sad, then angry in no particular order. When our children can experience our processing of emotions, they learn to process their own emotions. Obviously, I don't mean that you should use your child as a surrogate (that is covered in the next chapter). You should reserve most of your emotional heaviness for a time when your children don't bear the brunt of it, but it's okay and even healthy to let them in on your emotional state from time to time.

Grief Lies

As I was laying the foundation for this chapter, I was sitting in my favorite chair watching a storm roll in from the Gulf of Mexico—from the balcony of my very own beach house! I had officially accomplished making one of my dreams come true by myself (with God's guidance, of course). Had I not properly grieved my losses and moved to acceptance, I could have missed walking into the unbelievable story God had planned for my future. Today, I open my home and run beach retreats to help women heal after betrayal. I also do a little fishing on the side! What I grieved and feared at the beginning has not come true at all. I had not lost the whole beach—just the beginnings at the beach, and truly, those memories are not gone. They are a good reminder of precious times in my past. God redeems. He can help all of us move into a renovated life, but we have to participate by grieving our losses before we can welcome our new reality.

CHAPTER 4

No Surrogates, Please: Letting Your Children Be Children

Let them be little.

Billy Dean

Brittany reluctantly plopped on the sofa of the therapist's office.

I wish I could manage this anxiety on my own, she thought to herself. *It doesn't even make sense . . . I should be able to figure this out myself.* Her therapist, Shannon, poked and prodded into areas that Brittany hadn't thought about for years.

Shannon opened with, "Tell me about your childhood."

Brittany quickly responded, "It was great! My mom and I were close. We were a normal family."

Shannon prodded, "When did you say your parents were divorced?"

"When I was nine, my brother was six, and my sister was four," answered Brittany. "We were close. I was a 'little mommy,' and my mom and I talked about everything. Yes, my mom trusted me to tell me all about her troubles."

Shannon was struck by how unsuspecting Brittany was: she had no idea that it wasn't her job to listen to her mother's problems. Brittany thought it was normal to have heard everything about her father's affairs at the age of nine.

She explained, "Once, I was told to call Daddy and tell him that he needed to come home to the family because Mama was in bed and couldn't get up because of a bad headache. Mama always had headaches. I knew how to iron, how to cook meat patties, and how to do laundry at an early age; it was my job."

Brittany didn't know that other nine-year-olds didn't do those things. She thought it was normal. What she did know is that she had always dealt with a strong feeling of inadequacy.

The Hierarchy of Parenting

The duties of childhood are play, explore, laugh, repeat. Throughout their developmental stages children learn how to move from being dependent to independent, and from irresponsibility to responsibility. This should develop slowly over time. Kids need to stay focused on kid things, like how fast they can go on their bike, how their dinosaur collection is growing, and how much bling they can wear as a princess. Their biggest care in the world should be how they can avoid their nighttime baths or how to hide the green veggies on their plates. But mostly, children should be free to let their imaginations run wild and lose themselves in a world of fun and games.

When adults share their issues with their children, they expose them to problems that a child's brain is not designed to handle. Adult issues are too big for a child's brain. Children's innocence is damaged when their parents use them as a waste dump for their emotions. Damage occurs when a child hears traumatic things, often including their other parent, too soon. Yet in therapy, we often observe parents who are so wrapped up in their own pain and anger that they cannot help but share it with their children. The emotional damage inflicted on the child can be irreparable. When a kid's innocence is adulterated, the young brain acclimates by cooperating with being a caretaker, fixer, and/or hero. In fact, it becomes a way for the child to survive. Subconsciously, the child believes, "I must listen to Dad to make him feel okay so that he can be okay to take care of me." This people-pleasing survival response is not easily undone in adulthood. The child may grow up to become a peacekeeper—to his or her own detriment, because it is virtually impossible to keep the peace all the time when other parts are involved. Each person has his own free will. We can only be responsible for our own internal peace. Children exposed to too much adult drama may be set up to feel like they have to do something to make peace, which is harmful and can have lasting effects on their brains and future functioning.

In extreme cases, children are subjected to emotional incest—a dysfunctional scenario in which a parent looks to the child for emotional support. Just as the name implies, it is an improper relationship between parent and child that exploits the child. Here's how author Susan Peabody describes it:

A parent is lonely and turns to the child for support. The child becomes the adult emotionally, and the adult becomes the child. The parent and child are best friends. The parent and child are emotionally enmeshed. There are no healthy boundaries. They used to say "smothered"; now they say "emotional incest."[1]

For some, a sense of shame or the belief that "what happens in our home stays in our home" keeps them from getting outside help. Others have been burned in the past, so trusting another soul with their struggles is out of the question. These individuals often pull inward and hold in their pain until it ekes out around their children. These contributing factors make it tempting to lean on their kids as an emotional outlet. Whatever the reason for keeping the emotion confined to the nuclear family, consider reaching out beyond the confines of your walls for aid.[2]

Let the Children Come to Me

The Bible has a lot to say about parents' responsibility of disciplining and raising their children. "Train up a child in the way he should go, and when he is old he will not depart from it" (Proverbs 22:6 RSV). Children are referred to as righteous and innocent, not yet blighted by the travails of this life. In Matthew 18:2–6, Jesus calls us to protect their innocence:

> And calling to him a child, he put him in the midst of them and said, "Truly, I say to you, unless you turn and become like children, you will never enter the kingdom of heaven. Whoever humbles himself like this child is the greatest in the kingdom of heaven. Whoever receives one such child in my name

receives me, but whoever causes one of these little ones who believe in me to sin, it would be better for him to have a great millstone fastened around his neck and to be drowned in the depth of the sea."

The purity and naiveté of childhood is the basis for a child's need for protection. This stern warning suggests that harm against the righteousness, or pure innocence, of a child should be taken seriously.

We must be keenly aware of our children's emotional capacity and protect them from concerns they were never meant to bear. Causing disturbance is the opposite of comforting our children, and the Bible warns against it (Colossians 3:21). Find your own outlet for your emotions and let your children be guileless, the way God intended.

Remember the story about Brittany at the beginning of this chapter? She finally surrendered to the idea of counseling because she couldn't sleep at night and suffered gastrointestinal issues and occasional panic attacks. She couldn't make the correlation between her childhood of caretaking her mother and siblings with her current anxiety and depression. Through therapy, Shannon helped Brittany discover how to say no to others, how to discover what she enjoyed doing, and how to recognize her inner voice and emotions. How about you? Are you ready to take these next steps, too?

How to Get It in Order

The antidote to making your child a surrogate is getting support elsewhere. Look into divorce support groups or Bible studies where you can make safe adult connections with others in similar circumstances. Strive to lean on your support systems instead of your children. Break free from staying private about your pain. Make that appointment with a therapist and let them bear some of your emotional burden. Journaling your pain will also help immensely. Allow yourself time to process your emotions, then join your children in their childhood. Take them swimming, hiking, bike riding, read a book with them, engage in fantasy and play time with them. Be silly and let them be silly. Help them live out their job responsibilities in a fun way! Give children what they are asking for, but don't give them too much information. They are great about telling you when you have said too much. Watch for their cues, including tuning out, shutting down, getting angry, or worrying for you. Change the subject, apologize for saying too much, and then encourage them to be kids.

How Controlling Yourself Helps Your Child

In psychology, a concept called internal locus of control describes how people see their own success through the lens of their talents and abilities. Therefore, they feel like they have control of their lives. They have choices, can trust themselves, and trust that their internal voices will express their needs. Those with an external locus of control, on the other hand, look to others to define their happiness and make decisions for them. These individuals often feel that their own lives are out of their control. Children who are forced to bear adult problems learn early on that if Mom or Dad isn't happy, no one is happy. They begin believing that it is their job to make everything okay, but their emotional immaturity can lead them to become "extreme peacekeepers." They can feel ultra-responsible for maintaining peace everywhere, at all costs— even (and especially) to the denial of self. When a parent doesn't understand his behavior's impact on his child, the child internalizes the idea that his own feelings don't matter, or must be subjugated to his parent's feelings, which can lead to a codependent lifestyle. Ultimately, the child's own emotions become suppressed, and he learns to pacify and hold space for others in order to survive.

Does any of this ring a bell? Do you sense dysfunction on the home front? It's time to take your rightful role as a parent and let your children be children! Parents are the caretakers and should create a safe, protective space in the home for their children. Remember the pecking order of caregiving versus care receiving. Bottom line: your children should not be holding space for your emotions. You should be holding space for theirs. It is ultimately neglectful to get this out of order. Chapter 17 will discuss just how important being emotionally present for your youngsters really is.

Be the Change

If you have made a mistake in this area, stop and forgive yourself. And then take a good long look at what deficits in your life have caused you to view your children as peers. Most likely, it is a lack of adult connection. Get into a support group and start creating a healing team for yourself to have an outlet for your emotions. Above all, give your children permission to be kids.

Here's another important step: consider apologizing to your children and asking for their forgiveness. The good news is that you can arrest the problems of people-pleasing and caretaking if you address them with your kids. Making amends can teach our children that adults make mistakes and can learn to change their behavior. Do-overs are a great concept to initiate in the home and send perfectionism packing! You can be a part of changing the pattern, even if you were the one to cause it. Now, that is redemption!

Teaching your children that they don't have to take care of you will enable them to learn to take care of themselves. As a single parent, you might feel tempted to say, "What the heck does taking care of yourself even mean?" Read on for the answer.

CHAPTER 5

Put on Your Own Oxygen Mask: Practicing Self-Care

Rest and self-care are so important. When you take time to replenish your spirit, it allows you to serve others from the overflow. You cannot serve from an empty vessel.

Eleanor Brown

"**S**tacey, you should take a weekend off or you should go get a massage."

During the season of my divorce, I would balk and say, "I can't do that, the kids come first."

During my journey of healing, I began attending Al-Anon meetings, where a seasoned veteran told me, "Honey, you put God first, then yourself, then others." I was flabbergasted! Hadn't she learned in church the old dictum, "The way to joy is Jesus, others, and *then* yourself"? I thought my mentor had it all wrong. As it turned out, she was absolutely right. I was exhausted, totally at the end of my rope, and resenting all I *thought* had to do. I was missing a key ingredient: self-care. Eventually, I began to see that when I took care of myself, I felt happy and energized. The resentment faded away. I was more productive and less "busy."

Today, along with taking care of many clients, I am the caregiver for my ninety-eight-year-old mother, who lives with me. I've noticed that she does well when I give her constant attention: cook her meals, brush her hair, and visit with her daily. But I can't do that 24/7. Whenever I take time to go to my happy place, the beach, my mom suffers, which is painful to watch. For a few days, she becomes foggy, depressed, and a bit confused. It's often tempting to heed her affection for my presence and not go take care of myself. Yet I know that I have to take care of myself in order to take care of her. When I return recharged from the beach, I gladly make her fried bananas in the morning and dutifully get her nightly order of a McDonald's cheeseburger and a small vanilla shake (no whip). They know me there. $3.25 every time. I do it with a smile and gratitude that I still have my mom, because I know, as Momma says, "You'll fly away again soon and then come back to light for a while before you take off again." She calls me the high-flyer. She says it with a smile, and again, I am grateful that she gives me the space to take care of myself. Not everybody will be so gracious. Not everyone will understand your need for self-care. That is okay. Do it anyway!

Self-Care

As a single parent, you are your household's CEO. Your mood affects everyone in the home. When the boss is grumpy, the employees get the fallout! Do you get the idea? You are worth taking care of, and this will benefit you and your children immensely. It is important to gauge how you are feeling on a daily basis. It is your responsibility to monitor your energy level—your emotional battery—and to recharge when necessary. Know what fuels you and helps you to face another day. When you do this, you show your children that you are worthy of care, self-respect, and balance. They will learn that they don't have to be superheroes all the time to be acceptable. Even though today's culture doesn't often model this for us, there is truly a science behind self-care.

Autonomic Nervous System

Stress and fatigue are real issues for single parents. When the brain is stressed, it prepares the body to meet the perceived oncoming challenge. The heart rate increases, breathing becomes more difficult, and muscular tension/tingling and cold sweats occur. This aroused state sends the body into a "ready for battle" stance that helps us fight whatever we are up against. The autonomic nervous system is responsible for bringing the body back into balance. Specifically, the parasympathetic nervous system creates conditions to allow the body to rest and digest after a stressor. A sense of safety must be regained in the body. These activities of self-care—regular sleep, eating, exercise—are essential to physiological health.[1]

You can improve your own well-being by initiating the processes within your body that send messages of safety to your brain. As a therapist, I cannot write pharmaceutical prescriptions, but I do prescribe self-care to my clients. I tell them that it is not a luxury or a trendy little idea, but a neurobiological necessity for mental and physical health. It sounds crazy for me to tell you to remember to eat healthfully, take time for exercise, and get seven or eight hours of sleep— but often, these are the first things abandoned when people become single parents. The absence of another adult in your life should not keep you from taking care of yourself! The more you practice self-care activities, the more your brain is habituated to doing them. I liken it to a well-worn path on a ski slope. Your brain gets used to going down the black diamond slope of hazards, obstacles, and challenges where the pace is fast, furious, and forceful. When you train your brain to choose the nice, easy green slope, a new neuropathway or groove in the snow is established. The brain does not like negatives, so if it has an alternative, it will choose the path of least resistance. I have retrained my brain so that it craves peace more than it craves chaos. I used to pride myself on doing the next thing and the next thing and the next thing. Now my brain screams, "Go take a walk and relax!" and I graciously acquiesce!

Being Still

Christian self-care starts with knowing Jesus. How do we know Him? By being still (Psalm 46:10). Often, when I'm involved in some sort of self-care routine, I start to hear His voice and feel His peace. The ultimate goal of the Christian life is knowing God and finding peace. Nowhere in the Bible does it tell us to push ourselves, run ragged, or burn the candle at both ends. In fact, the Word instructs us to do the opposite:

> Do not conform to the pattern of this world but be transformed by the renewing of your mind. Then you will be able to test and approve what God's will is—his good, pleasing and perfect will. (Romans 12:2 NIV)

When we are constantly active, we are not renewing our minds. That comes when we rest and digest. This is part of the parasympathetic nervous system and is the biological opposite of the fight-or-flight response of the sympathetic nervous system. When we are still, our bodies can recoup from stressors and begin to calm down and feel safe. Being a single parent comes with a long list of job responsibilities. Your instinct may be to check every box to feel like you are competent. However, maturity knows that merely punching the list does not make you feel like you're enough. Check yourself in this area of perfectionism. You are enough in Christ, without doing one thing. When you base your ideas of performance on that identity, you can achieve a much more balanced approach to managing your life. As Robert McGee states in his classic book *The Search for Significance*,

> The focus of the Christian life should be on Christ, not on self-imposed regulations. Our experience of Christ's lordship is dependent on our moment-by-moment attention to His instruction, not on our own regimented schedule.[2]

Let's face it: it is tempting to be stringent in order to function as a single parent. However, in your diligence, try not to get locked into performance to the point of being consumed by it. Evelyn, a young, newly single mom, dreaded Back to

School night. She was exhausted from her job as a CEO. And she was newly divorced. She felt like she had a giant D on her chest announcing her new status. Her first instinct was to push through as usual, but it was all too much. As she suffered under the stress of it all, a solution occurred to her. *I can take care of myself and choose not to go this year,* Evelyn thought. She had learned a lesson about the importance of self-care and was exercising her right to choose what was best for herself. She knew that her emotional reservoir was empty and wisely chose to stay at home and do yoga for an hour. It would have been easy for Evelyn to give in to being Wonder Woman and say, "I can handle it!" Or even go on the head trip of *A good parent goes to Back to School night* (or *What will people think if I don't show up?* or *My children will think I don't care about them if I don't go*). These common ruminations can overpower the still, small voice inside that says, "No, I can't handle that tonight." By staying balanced, Evelyn held on to herself and her limitations. She was calm and even-keeled at home, finding gratitude in her time with her children. Running too hard or too fast can cause resentment.

Can you relate to Evelyn? If you feel resentful for all you have to do, it's a good bet that you're doing too much. It's time to try a little self-care. These should get your mind headed in the right direction.

Self-Care Formulary

1. Say no
2. Take a hot bath
3. Leave work early
4. Diffuse calming essential oils
5. Light a candle
6. Shave your legs and use great-smelling lotion
7. Shave yourself with a new aftershave
8. Play a round of golf with your buddies
9. Join a Bible study group
10. Enjoy your favorite meal
11. Read a book
12. Take a night out with friends
13. Take a long walk or run
14. Invest in a hobby
15. Take a nap
16. Take a vacation

Let Your Children Witness Your Rest

When you take care of yourself, you demonstrate that you are worthy of being cared for. This models self-esteem for your children. They learn that it is healthy to take a break to enjoy life. When parents push and push, kids begin to believe that achievement—or even worse, "busyness"—is the only thing that makes them worthy, and anything else is frivolous. Remember, those kids are watching every move you make and taking notes on what to do in their own life. The note taken when a parent never slows down is *I must achieve to be worthy of love.* As you do more and more, your pedestal ascends higher and higher, making it harder for your children to live up to your legacy. This is a recipe for raising a performance-driven child who grows into an adult that fears failure.

Understand this: others are affected by your mood. They watch and take cues from how you enter the home. They ask themselves, "Is it safe to approach? Should I walk on egg-shells? Can I take up space here? Is there room for my emotions?" There is a dance among family members regarding emotional space in the home. You are the director of the dance. It is your job to decide how the dancers attain equal space. This means that your needs must be taken care of for you to be objective and empowered. When you accomplish this, the dance is smooth and easy and represents balance to your children.

Go to the Pharmacy

Think of this chapter as a self-care prescription. Now, it's time to fill it. Decide what first small step you will take, and then muster up the courage to take it. It always helps if you have accountability. Ask another single parent friend to check up on you, ensuring that you're taking care of yourself. It is easy to forget you need this care, but others can recognize this more quickly than you can, especially if you tend to overload yourself. Assemble your team and get to it. Relax, and enjoy it!

Taking good care of the temple that God gave you is important. The overall effect of balance between *go* and *stop* will determine your well-being. Inevitably, you will be concerned about the gaps left when you punch out of parenting for the day.

Next, we will explore how to invite God into that space, trusting that He can provide what you can't.

CHAPTER 6

God Is My Coparent: Receiving God's Guidance

God is our refuge and strength,
a very present help in trouble.

Psalm 46:1 KJV

"Lord, I just can't do this alone," I cried out to God as I zipped through traffic on my way to the grocery store. I was picking up snacks and drinks for my teenage daughter's get-together later that evening. She had invited a group of co-eds to watch movies, which caused my brain to reel with all kinds of catastrophic possibilities.

"I have no idea how to manage a room full of teenagers," I continued. "What if they try to couple up? What if they turn out the lights? What if . . ."

A wave of anxiety washed over me. "If I had a husband, we would be making these decisions together. I am alone and don't have anyone to help me." Suddenly, I began to descend into an ugly vortex of blaming God and lashing out at Him:

"Why didn't You save the marriage? Why am I in this space? This is so unfair!"

I pulled into a parking spot, took a deep breath, and stretched my hand out over the console of my Suburban as if to hold hands with an invisible person next to me. And then I whispered unexpected words that seemed to roll off my tongue—a heartfelt yearning that bubbled up to the surface: "God, will You be my husband?"

Finally, my true desire! The words hung in the air for a moment as I took another breath. And then I continued: "Would You be my coparent? Would You help me parent my daughter? Would You help me set ground rules? Will You put the right words in my mouth and give me the courage to be a single parent?"

In that moment I knew I wasn't alone. I would be partnering with the King of the Universe to raise my children.

Conscious Contact

Stephen

That crucial revelation—we are not alone, even though we may feel like it at times—changed the path Stacey was on. That breakthrough in her life brought her to solid ground, and it moved her one step closer to emotional healing. If you learn just one thing in this chapter (actually, this entire book), here's what it should be: God has not abandoned you, and He will lead your steps if you ask. But reaching out and asking is the key, just as Stacey discovered.

Start by assessing your *conscious contact* with God. In other words, examine how you connect with and seek direction from the Lord. I like how the Alcoholics Anonymous (AA) organization explains it in its guidebook, known simply as the Big Book. In the eleventh step of AA's popular twelve-step program, the Big Book states that connection with God is "sought through prayer and meditation to improve our conscious contact with God as we understood Him, praying only for knowledge of His will for us and the power to carry that out."[1]

Being conscious involves awareness and response. So far in this book, we've discussed the importance of being aware of our thoughts and emotions and responding appropriately. Similarly, it is essential that we stay in tune with God's promptings and move closer to Him. AA's eleventh step urges us to make a concerted effort to talk to God and to listen to Him on a regular basis. One danger of being a solo parent is the risk of becoming so independent that we forget we need the Lord on a daily basis, and that He is willing and able to help us. There's also a tendency for each of us to wallow in self-pity.

Give God the opportunity to hear your cry. Go ahead and unload all that you are burdened with and pour out your needs to Him. Share your fears, recount your inadequacies, and allow yourself to be vulnerable before God with all that is troubling you. Then open yourself up to hearing from Him.

Stacey felt amazing after she unloaded all her stress and began to seek God's direction. Her brain was then clear enough to be logical and to develop a plan to handle her situation. Above all, she knew God was with her. When she returned home and faced her daughter, she set clear boundaries and explained that she would be checking in on her and her friends. Stacey told her that it was her daughter's responsibility to share the boundaries with her friends as well. Later, after Stacey's first check on the group, all was as it should be. But on another "room surveillance," the lights were off and some of the couples were snuggled up under blankets. Stacey snapped on the lights and said something playful about no funny business. By the end of the evening, Stacey could let out a sigh of relief. Parenting mission accomplished, at least for one day out of the year. As for the 364 awaiting her—no sweat! God would be with her every step of the way.

A Truth for Every Doubt

Stacey

You'd be surprised by the number of Christian single parents who have a hard time trusting the One they say they follow. Yet as we look more closely at the different kinds of trauma in their lives, a clear picture emerges as to why they're so reluctant to seek and follow God. Sometimes they feel as if God has let them down when bad things have happened to them. (We often forget that God allows evil and that we are not immune to it.) And some have to work through strong feelings—even anger—toward God for not "telling them" their spouse was cheating. Others feel too busy to seek Him.

Here are some common doubts we often hear, along with some encouraging truths that can nudge us closer to Jesus.

Doubt: "God is not here physically."

Truth: "Even though I am not with you in person, I am with you in the Spirit." (1 Corinthians 5:3a NLT)

Doubt: "God doesn't care about my little problems."

Truth: "Look at the birds of the air; they do not sow or reap or store away in barns, and yet your heavenly Father feeds them. Are you not much more valuable than they?" (Matthew 6:26 NIV)

Doubt: "God doesn't understand."

Truth: "This High Priest of ours understands our weaknesses, for he faced all of the same testings we do, yet he did not sin." (Hebrews 4:15 NLT)

Doubt: "I can't feel God."

Truth: "Now faith is the substance of things hoped for, the evidence of things not seen." (Hebrews 11:1 KJV)

God is omniscient, omnipresent, and omnipotent. He knows all, He is right here, and He is all powerful. Fall into the Lord's open arms and let Him sustain you. Humble yourself in the sight of the Lord and He will lift you up (James 4:10). It all begins with surrender. Are you trying to do it all through your own strength? Are you ready to open yourself to His power and compassion?

We have great empathy for anyone who struggles to see, hear, and trust God. If this describes you, rest assured that you are not the first to doubt God's sufficiency when things look bleak. Flip through the pages of Exodus in the Old Testament and read about the Israelites who wandered in the desert. They weren't sure they would even survive their circumstances. Then manna started falling from the skies (Exodus 16). They knew what God had promised, but options were running out as the Red Sea trapped them in danger from the approaching Egyptians (Exodus 14). God parted the Red

Sea as Moses obediently raised his staff in faith. These are just two of the provisions in the Bible of God's care for His people. Jews recite these miracles to their children at Passover to remind them that God hears our prayers and saves us from our afflictions. As you familiarize yourself with Scriptures about God's provision, you'll begin to glimpse His character. One of the names of God is *Emanuel*, which means "God is with us." He is right there with us in the fiery furnace, in the desert, in our moments of despair. This truth flies in the face of thoughts like *I am alone*. So, grab on to God, who is there waiting to partner with you, and grasp the truth that ***you are not alone***!

The Pipeline to Connection

Shelley began with an earnest desire for God's guidance. In the first ten minutes of her morning, she purposefully got out of bed, opened her Bible to read one verse, wrote it down, and then committed that day to the Lord. That dedication advanced into a habit that grew in length and regularity. Soon, she was able to spend at least thirty minutes improving her conscious contact with God on most days. Shelley looked for every opportunity to meet with God. She put down her phone in carpool line and told God what she was grateful for that day. In the evening, when craziness rose to a fever pitch, she would escape to the bathroom, put in her AirPods, and listen to a praise and worship song ending with a short appeal, "God help me!" She was then able to resume the evening routine with a new attitude. Shelley also realized that she could have two hours to focus on God if she took advantage of childcare offered during a weekday Bible study at her church. Sometimes it takes creativity to find time to meet with God. Start somewhere and God will honor your effort. Don't get hung up on "shouldas" or "oughtas." Just get creative and find a way!

Think of your relationship with Jesus as a friendship. You start by talking to Him, telling Him about yourself, learning about Him . . . and letting Him help you. Here are some ideas to get you started in your communion with God:

- Talk to God like you would a spouse.
- Tell Him what you think about the issue at hand.
- Write letters to God.
- Make a prayer closet.
- Turn your car into a sanctuary.
- Turn carpool line into praise time.
- Listen to a sermon on a podcast.

- Make a God Box where you can leave your concerns.

Taking Refuge in the Lord

Maggie fell to her knees and sobbed to God. Her eighteen-year-old daughter, Jordan, had just come home to announce that she was pregnant by a guy who would not likely take any responsibility for the child. Maggie felt so alone. Her heart broke for her daughter's dashed dreams. Maggie feared that Jordan would never have a husband who cherished her, and that Jordan would never have the normal life that she wanted her to have. Maggie felt guilty, and even believed that it was her fault that Jordan had gotten pregnant, because she, too, had been an unwed mother. She also found herself mad at her daughter for choosing to sleep with such an unsavory character. As Maggie crumpled on the floor and cried out to God, she let the fears and tears flow. But in the midst of all her emotions, she began to feel God's presence. She sensed a peace when she remembered bits and pieces from her Bible study of First and Second Kings. She had learned how Solomon and other kings had allowed compromise to lead themselves to fall away from God. Maggie was able to forgive herself for own mistakes and give grace to Jordan as well. She realized that that Bible study, at that time, was no accident. God knew that she would need to trust Him during this heart-wrenching period, and that she would need the material from this study to aid her in the process. She began to thank Him and offer up praise. As she did, she realized that her church had a ministry for unwed mothers-to-be. After she grieved the fact that her daughter was one of them, she realized that this, too, was likely a provision from God. Her daughter had lately been pushing away from her faith and refusing to go to church. Maggie knew that connecting Jordan with this ministry while she was feeling so vulnerable and alone might just be her connection back to Him. Now Maggie was not feeling so alone, either. She started realizing that God was indeed stepping in to be her husband (Isaiah 54:5). He really had been all along, but she was just now discovering it.

The bonus of asking for help is receiving it. Your kids will notice as you draw strength and protection from the Lord, and they will respond by feeling safe and secure. As you speak about your spiritual journey with God, your kids will learn that you rely on Him for help. They will experience His competence to guide you as you guide them, in ways that bring safety and stability. You will develop confidence as He leads you to trust yourself or reach out to another person for insight.

Your children will benefit from that confidence by feeling like they are in good hands. You also teach your children about the wellspring of wisdom that comes from seeking God. One of our favorite verses is Jeremiah 2:13: "My people have done two evil things, they have abandoned me, the fountain of living water, and dug for themselves cracked cisterns that hold no water at all." Teach your kids to drink from this spring for wisdom, strength, and guidance by your example. This sustaining element is an unending gift that will guide them throughout their lives.

CHAPTER 7

A Faithful Provider: Receiving God's Provision

*God really does have it all worked out. The gaps are
filled. The heartache is eased. The provision is ready.
The needs met. Fully. Completely. Perfectly.
In Him. With Him. By Him.*

Lysa TerKeurst

A s I set out on my familiar route for my morning run, I
reviewed the day ahead. This new running routine had
started from a couch-to-5K program. By daily making me put
one small step in front of another, the routine was saving my
life. It worked! I was now running—and I am not a runner.
Sometimes, the night was so fitful, I was elated to see the sun
peeking through the blinds at me so I could leave my bed, which
had become a dreaded place of disturbance. So, I arose at the
crack of dawn to have some routine, some normalcy, something
I could control in my life. That day, as I strode step after step, I
recalled a conversation with my son. I had never had technology
before my family members, even my preteen to teenaged children. My husband had always had the newest gadget on the

market. However, I always landed on the prudent side of spending due to our financial difficulties. Now that I was separated, the church was helping us with finances. Friends were sending me random gift cards. When they collected for the Bible study books in my neighborhood Bible study group, my books were miraculously paid for, session after session, by an anonymous benefactor. These little blessings had excited my son.

"Mom!" said Zach. "If you sold your iPhone on Craigslist you could almost pay for a new one!"

The latest iPhone had just hit the market and was the new buzz. People were even standing in line to get this new gadget. My internal deliberations were along the lines of *Well, my phone is glitchy and it is dropping calls . . . no, that is too much money, I can't do it. That is such an extravagance, a brand-new iPhone, and I don't really need it.*

"Mom, seriously—you deserve it, just go do it!" insisted Zach.

I calculated and re-calculated. I researched Craigslist and compared the value of my old phone to the cost of the elusive technology. The difference was $32.38. I could manage to front the money to myself until my old phone sold, but it was risky. Back then, I needed every penny. My conversations with Zach were plaguing my mind as I jogged along. I had made up my mind the day before that I would go stand in line and bite the bullet the next day. But now, on my run, I was rethinking it all. *After all, I am a charity case right now. How would it look for me to go get a needless item?* I mused.

Just then, something caught my eye. A wad of money on the ground right in front of me. In one sweeping motion, I angled my knees, lowered my hand, scooped up the wad, stuffed it in my running bra, looked around for the owner, and kept running. The money had been dropped. No one was around. It was a residential neighborhood, but the bills just lay in the street.

I got home, pulled out the crumpled cash, and counted it. It was $32. Exactly. If I were chatting with you over a cup of coffee, I would pause and let that sink in. Exactly $32. I can't even write the words that express what my heart felt in that moment. It was as if God was bellowing out of the heavens, "I see you, Stacey. I love you! You are worth it!"

That moment stands as a testament to my worthiness in God's eyes, His provision for me in a dire situation, and an assurance that I could trust Him forever.

Lack Begets Provision

Stephen

What's lacking in your life as a single parent? (Apart from the obvious.) Possibilities include time, money, resources, career stability, or social interactions. When we want something badly enough, our minds can become absorbed with it. A mind that is absorbed in lack cannot connect fully. If single parents follow Matthew 6:33 and seek first the Kingdom of God, I truly believe that God will provide all they need. When your mind is preoccupied, you can't be emotionally present for your children. This is where the rubber meets the road for faith. One client, recently separated, was offered a job as "Spiritual Culture Director" of her estranged husband's company the very day he was fired. She later began running the company. God reminded me of another newly separated woman whose church swooped in to help her hire a lawyer. They also fixed her car, and when it was beyond repair, assisted her in getting a new one. People in the church community provided financial and career help and even an AAA membership. Patty, a single mom of one, had been a professional before parenting. But when she became stunned by trauma, she couldn't think clearly enough to begin a job search, let alone have an interview. As she continued to seek God and work on her recovery, day by day, she yearned for the creature comforts that she could not afford. She surrendered her desires to God, and lo and behold, He used the NextDoor app to provide her a fire pit, a lamp, and a desk at a drastically reduced price. The very things she let go, God provided.

God Helps Single Dads, Too

Studies show that single-father families are better off financially than those headed by single mothers.[1] But men are not immune to financial fears. Often, the child support they owe feels cumbersome to them—a little like the old country song, "She got the gold mine, I got the shaft." I've heard men struggling with how to meet the endless needs of their children, fearing that they might somehow fail their kids. Men are also less likely to accept government assistance or seek support from agencies that offer it.[2] It doesn't mean that the need is not there.

A single dad may realize that he doesn't know what to do with a young woman growing up in his home. He certainly can't provide in exactly the same ways a mother could. This is an opportunity for him to take his concern to God, who can provide wisdom and insight into parenting a teenage girl, maybe in the form of a female mentor for his daughter.

Jehovah-Jireh

Stacey

When your children see you trusting God to provide everything, they learn about God's character. *Jehovah-Jireh* means "God is our provider." Abraham's Old Testament experience of his willingness to sacrifice his son Isaac to God is the basis for this characterization. You may not be putting your children on God's altar, but you will likely surrender some conditions concerning them. Maybe it is letting go of worry about a child's learning disability and believing that God will provide the right interventions for him or her. Perhaps you learn to let go of fretting that you won't be able to afford that select baseball team that your child qualified for. We see the faithfulness of God to Abraham and Isaac through generations, even to the lineage of Christ. We are all part of this story. Watch and see how God uses your submission to Him in His bigger picture.

Look for opportunities to teach your children, in parable-like stories, of your own experiences. Those can be interspersed with Bible stories of care and favor from God. Teach your kids about the lilies and the larks, the beauty of each bud, and how provision for pollination produces beautiful blooms. Recite to them then the wonder of the birds of the air never wanting for food or shelter (Matthew 6). As you weave those stories with your own reports of lack that has been fulfilled (even in very minute ways), your children will begin to have eyes to see God and His care even in the smallest things. What a gift to teach your children to praise God for His favor! When you do so, you are also strengthening their sense of security.

If they become anchored in the security of the God of the universe, what shall they fear?

Tools for Success

The key here is the opposite of picking up a tool. Instead, it is in letting your own unhelpful solutions go.

- Worry: "I can never make it alone."
- Fear: "What if someone breaks in?"
- Hyperbole: "My life is over!"
- Discouragement: "I can't get a job."
- Manipulation: "I will make her sorry she ever divorced me."

Pick up these tools and characteristics of waiting for provision.

- Trust: "I trust God to provide."
- Turn it over: "Lord, I give my concern to You."
- Let it go: "I give up the need for my kids to be in private school."
- Pray: "Help, God, I need You!"

- Tell God your need: "I need someone to help me move."
- Tell others of your lack: "I need help taking the kids to school."

Watch God Work: Eyes Open! Expect It!

Your need is not too big for God. James 4:2–3 instructs us to ask God for what we need. I see it like a game of catch. You catch the ball and throw it back. Wait and catch the ball again, then throw it back. Ask, let it go, wait. Ask, let it go, wait. Ask, let it go, wait.

My client Pamela was fleeing an abusive man in her workplace. She had become unproductive due to the harassment she experienced. Her car was repossessed, she couldn't afford her rent, and bills were piling up. Pamela began doing what she could do. She sold her designer luggage, her expensive belt, and her couture handbag. She admitted her plight to a new friend who had shared a similar story. This friend gave her money to reclaim her car. She spoke to the management company of her apartment, who delayed payment of her rent under provisions for hard times during the COVID-19 pandemic. One by one, Pamela's needs were met as she prayed to God for help and was honest with others about her plight. She gave glory to God as He accommodated each of her concerns.

Move Out of Fear and into Faith

You have heard these stories of God's faithfulness. Claim them as possible in your own life. Move out of fear and worry. Look past your circumstances and believe that God will provide for you. Ask for prayer, tell others of your concerns, and seek help and ideas for your situation. Claim God's promises:

> Do not be anxious about anything, but in every situation, by prayer and petition, with thanksgiving, present your requests to God. (Philippians 4:6 NIV)

> And God is able to bless you abundantly, so that in all things at all times, having all that you need, you will abound in every good work. (2 Corinthians 9:8 NIV)

> Who provides food for the raven when its young cry out to God and wander about for lack of food? (Job 38:41 NIV)

The thief comes only to steal and kill and destroy; I have come that they may have life, and have it to the full. (John 10:10 NIV)

But seek first his kingdom and his righteousness, and all these things will be given to you as well. (Matthew 6:33 NIV)

If you, then, though you are evil, know how to give good gifts to your children, how much more will your Father in heaven give good gifts to those who ask him! (Matthew 7:11 NIV)

And my God will meet all your needs according to the riches of his glory in Christ Jesus. (Philippians 4:19 NIV)

Compare. I was young and now I am old, yet I have never seen the righteous forsaken or their children begging bread. (Psalm 37:25 NIV)

So do not worry, saying, "What shall we eat?" or "What shall we drink?" or "What shall we wear?" For the pagans run after all these things, and your

heavenly Father knows that you need them.
(Matthew 6:31–32 NIV)

Now, sit back and watch God work! Part of receiving from God is receiving from others. God can use anybody or anything He wants to sustain and serve you. Let Him. Let them.

CHAPTER 8

It Takes a Village: Receiving from Others

Go quicky alone or farther together.

African Proverb

"God is going to give me the strength to handle all of this craziness!" Tomasa told me one day. For the past couple of years, she had been dating an amazing man named Arthur, who was ready to be a stepfather to her children. Arthur was a good dad to his own kids, engaged, empathetic, and involved. When he proposed to Tomasa on Christmas, she wasn't completely surprised, but was hesitant about remarrying. Yet, as she warmed to the idea, she began to see how God might be providing Arthur to her as a helpmate. She was the CEO of a company and had three children, one of whom had special needs. After others started mentioning that Arthur seemed like a long-awaited respite for Tomasa, she began to recant her independent warrior cry of "I can do this!" and admitted that help would be nice.

Do You Have an Aversion to Receiving?

Stephen

The Bible tells us, "God loves a cheerful giver" (2 Corinthians 9:7), but what about a cheerful receiver? Why is it so hard to ask for what we need? Why is so difficult to receive from others? Because asking and receiving are vulnerable behaviors that set us up to be hurt. Some people struggle to ask for help because of pride. Do you ever find yourself parading about like a three-year-old with an attitude of "I can do it all by myself!"? When we have been burned by others, we learn to become independent. When we have had to make do by ourselves, we become determined to not admit our weaknesses. But in doing so, we deprive ourselves of the gifts of teamwork, collaboration, and community. It is common for people who have had abusive backgrounds to fear rejection. This is completely understandable. The problem is, people who adopt this mindset decide to depend only on themselves. This thinking doesn't bode well for parents who find themselves single.

All children have needs that are beyond our ability to fulfill. It is our responsibility to understand where help from others would serve them best. If you are a dad parenting a daughter, find women who would be willing to act as mentors as she navigates growing up. When I was a single parent, I made sure that female friends attended my daughter's sixteenth birthday. I knew that I couldn't do it all as a father, so I rounded up a troop of six amazing women I admired to speak into my daughter Madeline's life. This gave her a network of support if she needed female advice, guidance, or a shoulder to cry on. What if my pride had gotten in the way and I insisted, "All she needs is me"? My child would have been deprived of a wealth of resources to aid her in her maturing. Instead, I wanted to give her a sage sounding board when she most needed it. The same holds true for mothers parenting boys. What a gift to give your son: a group of men to help teach him manhood. Sadly, Stacey never could create this for her teenage son. But it was always a prayer of hers. Now, eight years after her divorce, she sees God answering that prayer, exposing her son to strong men who offer a masculine perspective.

But what if they see our mess? We often fear that people will see us undone and unzipped. Here's some stress-relieving advice: So what if they see your mess? That old shaming belief may creep in, and we may fear that if they learn the real us, they won't accept us. We act like we are putting on a good show and that everyone thinks we have it all together. But consider this: Do you really think people expect you to have it all together? The answer is often a resounding no. Letting go and letting it all hang out allows help to enter—and that's a big relief.

Stronger Kids

Stacey

America glamorizes the caricature of the two-parent family where children are the flourishing center of attention. But the stereotype of single-parent, latchkey kids suffering alone at home isn't the norm, either. These misconceptions keep us from seeing the great possibilities available to us in asking for help. Children from single-parent families that welcome others to invest in their lives can and do thrive.[1] By embracing the "it takes a village" mentality, we expand the horizons of help for our children. Most successful solo parents utilize a wide variety of friends, relatives, educators, and neighbors to support their children. By sheer numbers, the more folks investing in our offspring, the more support our children will have, and the more they will feel championed and loved.

So often, we don't recognize that we need help *before* we become overwhelmed. In a popular blog post, parenting expert Matilda Chew writes,

> Even before it becomes too much, we need to have the clarity of mind and wisdom to allow others in . . . others who can help with baby-sitting when you would just like to take that shower, others (such as teachers and mentors) who help to teach your child what he/she needs to move forward and upwards in life, peers who provide friendship to your child and friendship groups which helps with identity and social development, and those who play a part in assisting with your child's moral/spiritual development.[2]

Faith Foundation

We know that we are urged to bear one another's burdens, and in doing so, we fulfill Christ's purposes (Galatians 6:2). This implies that everyone has burdens. What happens when a body of believers gather to work as a team? Loving, supporting, and completing a mission together creates what God had in mind to fulfill His plans. That is the essence of the special nature that the Bible refers to as *koinonia*—fellowship of believers. God created us with needs. He created Adam to need help from another person. He created Eve as Adam's helpmate. Therefore, asking for help is not admitting failure, but becoming aware that this is the way God made us. His provision for Adam shows us that He is faithful to fulfill our needs.

Icy, Dicey Times

"Admit it, Mom, we are cursed!" shouted Kayla as she clung to Vonda in the middle of the winter storm. "Look!" Kayla cried as she exhaled deeply. The droplets of water from her breath condensed in the cold air, and a misty cloud escaped from her mouth. Kayla and her mother had just returned to their sub-freezing house and opened the garage to a tsunami of water. They ran inside to witness a waterfall cascading from the second-floor balcony. Kayla's brother and father appeared to be unscathed by the storm, as their home was connected to the local hospital electric grid. Kayla had not been invited to seek refuge with her own father. No wonder she felt cursed. Providentially, troops of neighbors and friends from church worked tirelessly for five hours to get the water shut off and cleared out of the house.

One of the neighbors, who taught welding at the local state tech school, fixed the burst pipe. Church members brought industrial carpet cleaners and fans to remediate the damage. Vonda made a list of all their blessings and shared them with Kayla. They agreed that they were not cursed, not alone, and were very loved and supported. As one of Vonda's support group members noted, "None of this would have happened if Vonda had not cast all that bread on the water through her precious service and giving through the years." Vonda had laid the groundwork for creating a village for herself and her children by serving others and making connections that would sustain them in a time of need.

Here are some ideas to create community for your kids:

1. Home school co-op group: Let other parents help you in a teaching role.
2. Team sports: Allow the coaches to encourage and sharpen your young athlete.
3. Boy/Girl Scouts: Scoutmasters and helpers can encourage your kids through their badge earning and trips.
4. Youth group: Adult leaders and youth ministers can speak into your child's spiritual life.

5.   Mentors: Consider opposite-sex role models, such as other single parent friends, to speak into their lives.

6.   Teen mentors: Seek out older teens who will help shepherd your children in a positive direction.

7.   Big Brothers and Sisters: This organization finds mentors for kids from all walks of life.

8.   Family members: Think of aunts, uncles, and cousins who might be willing to take your child to fish, shop, or do things that you don't really enjoy.

Teamwork Makes the Dream Work

There is nothing quite like being on a team. Whether it is the Houston Texans, the local Boy Scout troop, or the Bible study group at church, being part of a group of people is magical. When one member is suffering, he or she is not alone. The others can and will pick up the slack. As you begin to bring others into your children's lives, your children will feel the supportive village mentality. They will feel ensconced by options for love and care. We don't want our kids to feel lonely and disconnected. Although kids can and should create connections on their own, why wouldn't we help build peer and adult support mechanisms for them?

Do you remember the game show *Who Wants to Be a Millionaire?* On that popular quiz program, if a contestant got stuck, he was given three lifelines. Two of those lifelines were phone a friend and ask the audience. Don't we all need a lifeline? We all need a little outside help now and then! Use your lifelines. Create lifelines for your children so that you are not their only resource. Use the power of the team, of community, to raise your children up into self-sufficient, confident adults. Renounce the self-sufficient persona and create a large sanctuary and refuge for your children. They will be better for it!

I was in college when my father died. I not only received a floral delivery from my own sorority, but all the sororities on campus sent me flowers as well. From 250 miles away, I felt their love and concern. I knew that when I returned to campus, they would be there to usher me back to normalcy with love, concern, and awareness of my tragic loss. This might seem small, but to me, it was an immensely comforting gesture. My father's death marked the beginning of my journey in a single-parent home. From the start, I felt loved and nurtured by my mom. It would have been easy to feel different or somehow substandard. However, neither of us really struggled with that. I had community and connection. If you are feeling like an oddball due to your singleness, read on to understand what to do about it.

CHAPTER 9

Misfit: Noticing the Discomfort of Singleness

Stephen

"Today's topic: how to strengthen your marriage!" bellowed the preacher.

With the words pelting her like jagged hailstones, with no stealthy way of escape, all Sandra could do was slink down in her pew. *Just kill me now*, she thought. *How am I going to sit through thirty minutes of this?*

The preacher continued: "Men, each one of you should treat your lady like the gem you know she is. Take the lead, invite her into prayer, do the dishes for her. She needs it!"

Sandra sank further as the pastor urged, "Men, lean over right now and put your arm around your bride, and let her know you are there for her!" As guys all around her scooted in tight to their wives, with their kids smiling widely at their parents' affection, Sandra couldn't hold in her emotion and began to weep. *If only I had this! I feel so alone—like I'll never have this kind of loving relationship. What does everyone think of me being here by myself?*

She believed her singleness stood out like a sore thumb against the paired-up couples in the sanctuary. Church suddenly felt unwelcoming for Sandra.

Awkward Feelings

It's little wonder that Sandra and so many other single parents feel like social misfits. Currently in America, 78 percent of parents living with children are married.[1] In other words, a majority of this group represents the quintessential nuclear family, compared to just 15 percent of parents living without a partner.[2] Mix in new research from Harvard sociologists suggesting that "neighborhoods with many two-parent families are much safer,"[3] and it's easy to see why some single-parent families feel as if they are on the outside looking in.

While the nuclear family is still common today, the structure of American households is changing and simply can't be defined the way it used to be.[4] Single-parent households are a valuable part of the mix, making them anything but misfits. In the remainder of this chapter, Stacey and I will explore those awkward feelings that plagued Sandra and so many other single parents.

First, have you ever gone into a restaurant and asked for a table for one? Some singles feel too awkward to eat alone. They don't know what they would do to entertain themselves without a partner to talk to. How about attending an event alone? In the early days after her divorce, Stacey was hesitant about going to her daughter's choir concert by herself. She feared finding herself in a triggering situation. In some ways, that caused her to feel small and insignificant, as if she wasn't enough all by herself. As we wade through all the emotional layers Stacey was sorting through, it pretty much boils down to grief. Worrying about the perceptions of others adds to feelings of grief and discomfort, and this anguish adds another layer to an already distressing situation. When singleness is new, it can feel awkward. And when we see ourselves as awkward, we feel incompetent. Then, if we worry about others' judgment, the situation can be so distressing that we retreat to isolation. That is the saddest outcome. In essence, it means being trapped by feelings of affliction, so you give up enjoying the things life has to offer. If you find yourself trapped in these feelings, notice them, and then go about trying to rationalize with yourself. Rational thought says that no one cares that much about you being solo. It says that you do have a place in this world. Sensible thinking also says that these events are what you make of them. The two keys to getting past the discomfort of singleness are time and practice. The good news is that Stacey's discomfort eventually passed, and today, she is confident and comfortable in her own skin.

Here's something else Stacey discovered: the more singles go places by themselves, the more comfortable they will feel. (We'll explore this in greater detail later.) As an added bonus, they will begin to enjoy the benefits of making their own decisions, free from the encumbrance of another's opinion.

You Are Not Alone

Feelings of uneasiness with being alone are very common, because we are all created for connection. We can look to stories in the Bible of people who went through periods of loneliness and discover that we are not alone. Leah (Genesis 29) always felt that Jacob had chosen her sister, Rachel, over her. Elijah (1 Kings 17) was exiled on more than one occasion. Wandering and away from home, surely he felt like an awkward misfit. Jeremiah was unmarried and experienced rejection. He wasn't called the "weeping prophet" for nothing.

Even King David spent time alone running from Saul (Psalm 142:4). And later, as king, he experienced all the power in the land, but may not have felt real connection and belonging. Finally, we remember the times Jesus Himself felt lonely. He must have felt disquiet in His soul, surrounded by people who didn't understand Him and later rejected Him. He verbalizes His anguish in Matthew 15:34, where He questions His abandonment by God. Even in the days before His death, He asked for companionship in the garden to pray, but He was left alone. During the Last Supper, He shared a meal with those who would betray him and deny him.[5] You are not alone in your loneliness.

Adventure

Stacey

I was beyond blessed to travel with New Life Ministries during my period of post-traumatic growth. I visited various locations throughout the United States to facilitate weekend healing workshops, and I found myself in some amazing places I'd never imagined I'd get to see in person. And yet, during one trip to Denver, gazing at the snowcapped Rockies from my hotel room, I was trapped by the limitations of my mind—a self-limiting belief that shouted *I must have a husband, or at least another person to travel with!*

I left that weekend with regret that I couldn't experience this beautiful city, because I didn't think I could do it alone. Maybe it was the shame of being single, or some fear about what people would think. Either way, I let my thoughts keep me from enjoying my life to the fullest. At that moment, I vowed that the next time I was there, I would strike out on my own to explore.

Several years later, I got the invitation to facilitate a group of people struggling with weight issues, again in Denver. I found a quaint little cottage motel with the most charming little stream running through it, as well as waterside fire pits. Done deal, I was there! I added two days to the front of my trip and spent those days hiking in the state park all by myself. The nights were spent sitting around the fire pit after a great dinner at a newly found restaurant.

Soon, I was tagging vacation days on the front end and back end of my trips. In Washington, D.C., I visited places like the Holocaust Museum, Arlington Cemetery, and the Capitol. I learned how to ride the subways and looked up the trendiest restaurants all by my lonesome. Now, every time I visit Southern California for a workshop, I look forward to my days in paradise at Laguna Beach. I always seem to end up there during restaurant week, and I indulge in specials that would delight the world's most sophisticated epicure. As I jog down the Pacific Coast Highway, I am energized as I encounter breathtaking views and discover nooks and coves that feel as though they were created just for me. I have found God waiting there for me on those journeys. I have discovered that I am never alone.

Have you ever thought about traveling alone? Some singles find it unreasonable even to consider that option. I learned to travel all by myself, and today, I appreciate the feeling of adventure I get when I discover new things, just for me and God! When the voices in your head scream *I am different! I don't fit in!* remember these statements below and ponder each one of them. Do this until the voice changes to *Let's go do this thing!*

Keys to Remember

Most people don't think you're strange for being alone. These thoughts are probably limited to your own head. It is doubtful that people are judging your solitude.

Start small. Take a walk. Visit a coffee shop. Just do the next thing that you want to do, alone. Just try it.

Take something to occupy your time. Bring a book, a journal, or some project to keep busy if you don't know how to fill up your time. A cell phone is another thing to resort to if you feel awkward.

Look for someone to meet. Peer out over your coffee cup and make a comment about the weather or their food. You never know who you will meet.

Remember that you can leave. You are not trapped. There is an exit door to every establishment. Give yourself grace if you get overwhelmed.

Consider the advantages of going solo. You get to choose all by yourself. You can stay as long as you want. You can leave when you want. You can sit wherever you want. You are the boss!

Choose something you love. Pick something that you get excited about, something that makes your heart sing!

I have to take a moment and speak to those of you who have young children at home. You are only wishing that you could take a trip as far away from those precious darlings as you could, *just to get a break!* But who in the world would keep all those kids for you, and how would you afford it? I get it. Maybe an adventure for you would be a trip to TJ Maxx alone! If you are lucky, you might be able to have a little bit of excitement attending your weekly Bible study and taking advantage of the free childcare. What makes you feel different is that you have young kids in tow, and some days, it feels like you are herding turtles. Don't let this challenging time define you. You are participating in an honorable, admirable endeavor that is of the utmost importance, and God has entrusted you to do it! If you get it, use the time that the kids are with their other parent to get used to going into public alone. (Unless, of course, you are busy napping!)

Open Up the World

When your children see you adjust to being single, they learn flexibility. They see that when life doesn't turn out as you imagined, you can still make the most of it. When you, in turn, see life with endless possibilities, their vision for their lives will broaden. You vicariously open up the world for them. My grown children get awfully jealous when they see the places I choose to visit and the things I get to experience. I think it has helped them dream and ask *why not?* for their lives and choices. My son announced last week that he and his bride were moving to another city five hours away. I wonder if my openness to explore and risk had some intrigue for him. On another note, we had a rare treat in Texas this month. It snowed in Central Texas! I happened to be in the middle of the uncharacteristic storm, and I sent gobs of snow-covered pictures to my daughter. Soon enough, she asked if the snow was steady and where I stored the cold weather gear. She struck out on her own adventure, driving three hours north-ward to enjoy the snow! I'd like to think that my kids' worlds have become big, open, and welcoming due to my own con-quering spirit.

Saying yes to singlehood, instead of feeling like you have to hide yourself, cuts the chains that bind you. Use some of the tools above to break free of grief and loneliness and dis-cover a whole new world out there. Use the opportunity to be the decider of your life. The world is your oyster. Go claim your part of it! If you happen to be stuck in the shame of singlehood, tack a sticky note to this chapter and read on. We will discuss the devastating effect of shame on your life and the bondage that it puts you in. But get ready to return to this chapter when you are free! You'll want to remember the adven-ture that is awaiting you when you drop the shame!

CHAPTER 10

The Scarlet Letter: Healing from Shame

Shame corrodes the very part of us that believes we are capable of change.

Brené Brown

"It was an unwanted divorce," I told others when I returned to church. I felt like there was a huge red D tattooed on my forehead after I was no longer married. I reeled against imagined judgment as I told my news to bewildered listeners.

Shame covered me like a thick blanket so that I was blinded to the truth. Shame kept me out of my favorite grocery store; I resorted to a lesser-known, fishy-smelling store to feed my family, because I knew no one there. In this out-of-the-way location, I felt a reprieve from the panic attacks that I felt on the side of town where I might run into the wrong people.

The shame was so irrational. I had done nothing wrong, yet it was keeping me in a prison of isolation and fear. I couldn't help it. It was a trauma response. I had crazy beliefs that had been wired in due to betrayal. Refrains of *I am not good enough* and *I am ugly* bore false witness to my inherent worth as a human being. I felt like I would never recover my self-worth.

The truth is, self-hate plunges us deeper into our struggles. It always begins with shame. We start feeling alone, isolated— way beyond God's love. *I'm a mess, a loser . . . simply no good and of no use to God.* These are all lies. In fact, if left to spin and swirl out of control, this whole line of reasoning—the toxic shame cycle itself—will eventually lead us to one place: destruction.

Thankfully, I found the help and hope I desperately needed once I embraced God's healing touch.

Killer Shame

Stephen

Maybe you are an unwed parent and your shame stems from judgments about having sex outside of marriage. Perhaps, like Stacey, you were betrayed, or your child's other parent didn't stick around and you feel abandoned. Maybe you are a widow or widower, and somehow, you believe that you are damaged goods because of your loss. Or, you may have chosen to parent on your own, but when you are quiet in the still of the night, voices of shame creep in, saying, *You are so stupid! What on earth were you thinking?*

Guilt relates to our behavior; shame relates to our identity. Guilt says, *I did something wrong*, while shame says, *I am something wrong*. Patrick A. Means explains it this way:

> When we do something wrong, our God-given con-science rings an alarm. That pang we feel is guilt. Guilt is not destructive to our person because we can do something about it. We can acknowledge our wrongdoing, change our behavior, experience forgive-ness, and we no longer have to feel guilty. . . . [Shame] pools and swirls outside the fringes of our lives like a poisonous nerve gas, waiting for us to open the door a crack and let it seep in to paralyze and destroy. Shame, in this sense, is a demotivator for ongoing growth. It usually results in self-condemnation, dis-couragement, and the urge to give up.[1]

God does not want us to live in shame. Plainly and simply, shame is not from Him! A favorite verse I quote to people stuck in crippling shame is 2 Corinthians 7:10, which says,

"For the sorrow that is according to the will of God produces a repentance without regret, leading to salvation, but the sorrow of the world produces death."

In his book *Untangling Relationships*, Pat Springle discusses this kind of crippling shame. He says,

> This guilt lacks objectivity about its causes and effects, and it is unforgiving. It promotes no love or acceptance, this guilt is a painful, gnawing perception that says, "I am worthless, unacceptable, and never can do enough to be acceptable no matter how hard I try, I am guilty of being a terrible person."[2]

Ask yourself this: *If the Creator of the Universe loves and accepts me and is ready to offer me grace, why am I allowing myself to remain in shame?*

Shame is the biggest killer of well-being. We see it daily in our counseling practices. We are big fans of Brené Brown,[3] a shame researcher at the University of Houston. Brown says in her TED Talk "The Power of Vulnerability" that three things make shame grow: silence, secrecy, and judgment. Shame drives us to isolation out of fear of judgment, and then it grows like an infection in a petri dish. The antidote to shame is connection. Once we bring our shame into the light, it can be exposed for the liar that it is! When we connect to others and share our deepest thoughts about ourselves, they begin to lose their power. This is one of the key reasons twelve-step support groups are successful for Alcoholics Anonymous. As members share, they usually feel accepted, and as they listen to others, they learn that they are not alone.

For those who wrestle with addiction, shame can send them back into the numbing substance or behavior that is their negative coping skill. The death of shame is the first step to breaking the addiction.

Three Portraits of Shame

Some of our Bible heroes hid in shame as well.

I am dirty might have been the belief of the woman with a bleeding problem in Luke 8:43–48. Imagine being known as "the bleeding woman." What a shame-based identity! In Jesus's time, uncleanliness meant uselessness. This woman was considered defiled, and therefore unfit to be around. Shame bound her and kept her in concealment. What brought her out of the darkness? Her daring act of faith. She risked touching the hem of Jesus's robe because she desired healing so much. This exposure to the Light immediately ended the problem that had kept her hidden. By exposing her shame, she was healed.

The Samaritan woman whose story is told in John 4 likely believed she was damaged goods. Feeling insignificant, she answered Jesus's request for water with her pronouncement of inadequacy to even be addressed by a Jew. She hid in the heat of the day to avoid the usual morning well-goers who cast judgment on women like her. Her emergence from hiding brought her to a fateful meeting with the Savior who brought her out of shame by His unconditional love and acceptance. She became a believer that very day.

If they knew the real me, they wouldn't accept me could have been David's cry after he slept with his soldier's wife. He then planned to have that soldier killed to cover up his indiscretion—sin covering sin because of shame and fear of judgment. David was guilty of committing adultery, but he didn't let it turn into self-defining shame. Later, David repented for his sin and was forgiven.

In the middle of their shame, these three biblical figures hid, but in the wrong places. They eventually learned to hide in the cleft of the rock (Exodus 13:22). Going to God and hiding in Him means being fully known, admitting failure, and leaning on Him for protection and righteousness.

Whether your shame stems from something that was done to you or a sin that you committed, the offer of forgiveness, healing, and truth is offered up to you from reaching out to

God. Dare to trust that He doesn't see you in the same light that shame has cast you in. Most of all, He wants you free!

But for the Grace of God, Go I

Stacey

Part of my practice is facilitating weekend groups for women who have experienced betrayal. During the first session, the women usually open up and tell their stories of how their husbands cheated on them. There are tears and empathy, and before the session is over, they have already bonded with each other.

At one weekend, as the second session was about to start, Gwen tracked me down. With a wild look in her eyes, she said, "Stacey, I can't go into that room with those women! I *am* the other woman! I had an affair with a married man. I can't let them know that!"

I inevitably have a Gwen in each group. I tell all of them that they need to go back into the group and tell the other women the truth. Most often, they protest and say, "They will hate me!" Shame causes them to be tempted to forgo their own healing and hide from an opportunity to grow.

I asked Gwen to trust me. In the next session, I called on her and told the group that she had something to share.

I always assure the group that sharing is safe and that we are learning a new way to listen and interact with each other. When Gwen told the group that she had an affair herself, I asked if anyone was triggered or needed to express anger or sadness.

Lisa was triggered, but when she saw Gwen's regret and remorse and heard her story, she softened. It was the most beautiful moment of grace when Gwen apologized to Lisa in a role-play scenario where grace and forgiveness were processed. Gwen's shame melted as the group accepted and loved her despite her admission. Lisa felt free from her anger. It was a win-win. Connection kills shame! This is powerful stuff! Every Gwen I have encountered has been hidden in her shame and freed when it is shared and grace is given.

Below are some practical ways to process this soul-crushing shame. I can't promise it will be easy, but I can say that it will be worth it.

1. Join a group.
2. Talk to someone about it.
3. Journal.
4. Talk to a pastor.
5. Hire a counselor.

Don't Hide

When you come out of hiding, a new life of freedom begins. Imagine living in the Witness Protection Program under a false name, in a new city, giving your kids new names. Think about having to always watch your back, worried that whoever you were being protected from was right around the corner. This would involve lying to cover up who you really are, in fear that people would find out the truth and your life would be in jeopardy. This is what living in shame is like. Now, imagine the day that the danger has passed, you can tell the truth, and you can return to your normal life. Envision the freedom that your family would feel to be themselves again. This is the freedom that is awaiting you and your family when you drop your shame and walk into being comfortable in your own skin.

Shame holds you in a prison of self-doubt. If you find yourself there, drill down and attack those lies. Our clients often seem like they have a ball and chain binding them to the therapy couch. They drown themselves in shame and self-limiting beliefs. After we work on these beliefs and expose them for the lies that they are, we watch in amazement as God frees them and removes their chains. We see it in their faces and hear it in their voices. This work we do is sacred. Indeed, it is a hallowed space to be in and watch God's healing work. You are worth the work. We will admit that it isn't always easy, especially if it has roots back into childhood (which is quite likely). Shame comes from so many different experiences in life. Satan uses these experiences to make us believe that we aren't worthy. Some of these beliefs can be reversed by replacing lies with God's truth. Others are so entangled that it takes the help of a therapist to become free. If you have even a mild set of events known as "little t" traumas, like emotional abuse, the death of a pet, bullying or harassment, or loss of significant relationships, EMDR (Eye Movement Desensitization and Reprocessing) can be helpful. After all, these aren't little to you! Invest in yourself. Get rid of this crazy killer called shame. Don't let it steal one more day from you or your children!

After my divorce, I sought the help of a professional counselor who employed EMDR to help my shame subside. EMDR uses bilateral stimulation of the brain through the use of eye movements to help the brain think more clearly and logically without so much emotion (we'll explain more about it in chapter 17). After EMDR treatment, I could shop the aisles of my Kroger, happily planning meals for my kids.

Shame can lead to a place of powerlessness and helplessness. It can render a person utterly paralyzed. If you find yourself thinking *It's not fair* or *There is nothing I can do about this*, you may have succumbed to thinking like a victim. If this sounds familiar and you find yourself stuck in this negative pattern, it is important to identify it so that it can be healed. We will discuss the victim mentality in the next chapter.

CHAPTER 11

Crippling Thinking: Rejecting Victimhood Mentality

A wise woman wishes to be no one's enemy; a wise woman refuses to be anyone's victim.

Maya Angelou

S ue Ann covered her face with her hands and rocked gently, sobbing uncontrollably. "I can't believe he left me," she said. "It's so unfair, after all I did for him—putting him through grad school, raising his kids. How could he do this to me?"

Her friend Allison listened patiently, occasionally rubbing her arm and offering a reassuring word or two. "I know, Sue Ann, it's just not right!"

The distraught woman looked up and squinted. "I want him to suffer!" she said. "I never thought I could have this much bitterness toward someone, but I really do. I want him to feel all the pain that's tearing me apart."

Sue Ann went on and on for what seemed like hours with various iterations of "It's not fair," "I have no choices," "My life is over," spewing out of her mouth like an exploding volcano. She belabored the fact that she could not make it on the measly child support that her ex was giving her and that she was getting behind on her bills. Yet Sue Ann refused to leave the large house with a pool where she raised her children. When Allison suggested downsizing, Sue Ann balked: "No way! He isn't going to take that away from me and the kids!"

Allison tried again by proposing that she get a job. Sue Ann shot down that idea, saying, "I can't do that! My children won't think I am there for them." Week after week, Allison listened and validated Sue Ann's pain, telling her, "I understand, this is difficult for you."

But Allison knew all too well that her friend was stuck in victim mode.

The Deep Freeze

What may have happened to you may really qualify you as a victim. There is no doubt that abuse, betrayal, gaslighting, or manipulation can be traumatizing. However, the mindset Sue Ann fell into, time after time, immobilized her and kept her from moving forward. Her paralysis set the stage for the entire mood of the house. Her children felt like they were imprisoned in a single-parent home without choices. As single parents, we must move into empowered thinking as we embrace our new lives. A huge benefit of being single is the power to choose for yourself. You get to make choices about your life, and you don't have to collaborate with anyone else.

In the remainder of this chapter, we'll dig deeper into what's going on emotionally. First, let's test your thinking to see if you are frozen in old habits or crippled by the fear of trying something new. Here are some signs of being stuck in victim mode:

1. Victim mentality: "poor me" thinking
2. "I can't" language: Looking at your glass as half-empty
3. Catastrophic thinking: Asking all the what-ifs
4. Taken advantage of: Lingering on the unfairness of it all
5. Incapable: Another form of "I can't"
6. Martyrdom: "Well, someone has to sacrifice. I guess it's up to me."

When we get overwhelmed and don't feel equipped to deal with our circumstances, our brains often go into victim mindset to survive. When we come up against something we didn't expect, we can feel helpless and powerless. This is a normal first stage of reacting to a stressor. We shut down to survive. What a wonderful survival mechanism God built into our beings! The protection from strong emotions allows time for the brain and body to absorb the new reality. However, if we stay in that victim mindset, we ultimately hurt ourselves and our children.

Another factor that keeps us in victim mode is the presence of something beneficial in that mindset. For example, increased attention from others may seem to protect against feelings of abandonment. After all, who could let down a poor single mom? Mathews explains,

> In this way, victims often bully others into all kinds of caregiving, running the gamut from providing financially for [the] poor victim, to literally making all of his choices for him. The victim typically knows exactly what buttons to push in others to get them to begin or continue to take care of him.[1]

I am not saying that this is everyone's intention. Quite the opposite is true. It can be completely subconscious. Often, this has been a modus operandi for a very, very long time, and could even be a survival skill developed in childhood.

The good news is that our brains can change! The brain has the ability to learn new information by forming new neural connections throughout life. This concept (neuroplasticity) means that you can move your thinking from a victim mentality to a victorious mindset. Nerve cells in the brain can respond to new stimuli and new thinking can result. Now, that is encouraging news! If you struggle to get out of this crippling mindset, it might behoove you to see a therapist and do the deep healing work that can change the way you think.

Here's more good news: You don't have to do it alone, because you have an Advocate! The Holy Spirit can empower you to do things that you cannot do on your own. So often, we forget that we are not alone on this single parent journey. Use the old saying "Fake it till you make it!" Put some encouraging verses all around your house, where you will see them every day. How about these:

- Philippians 4:13: "For I can do everything through Christ, who gives me strength." (NLT)
- 2 Corinthians 12:9: "My grace is sufficient for you, for my power is made perfect in weakness." (NIV)

- Deuteronomy 31:6: "Be strong and take heart and have no fear of them: for it is the Lord your God who is going with you; he will not take away his help from you." (BBE)

Recite these verses over and over until you believe them. This is what faith really is! Believe that you can lean on the Lord, and He will give you the courage to change the way you think. When we rely on our Advocate to stand for the injustices in our life, we can let go of the mindset of doubt, unfairness, and vengeance. This frees us to move into peace.

A New Normal

Stacey

One of my saddest thoughts about singlehood was losing my family holidays with big Martha Stewart meals, kids poking their heads into the kitchen, long-held traditions, and lots and lots of family around. After I grieved the fact that my holidays would not look the same, I set out to choose what I wanted them to become. My family had been fractured as the result of my divorce, and I had a deep fear that I would find myself alone.

I remember a specific Easter, early after my divorce, that shifted my fearful thinking into a growth mindset. I invited another single-parent family over for dinner. While these folks weren't my blood relatives, we enjoyed a wonderful meal together and spent the afternoon with people we loved. The best part is that we had created a family that we chose for ourselves and wanted to be around. I was overjoyed when my daughter came to me and said, "Mom, this is our new normal."

As we begin to shift into acceptance of our circumstances, we come into agreement with God that events are playing out the way they're supposed to. Our kids sense our resiliency, and they become resilient themselves.

The next month was Mother's Day, and since the Easter celebration had gone so well, we again gathered around my dining room table with the same family. The kids happened to be the same ages as my kids and were good friends. We invited another one of their friends over and began a game of true confessions around the dinner table. As we laughed and laughed, the hours ticked by, and the game changed to expressing what we were grateful for. This led to our children telling us what they loved and were grateful for about us as moms. I tearfully recorded that significant day in my mother's journal. It still stands as an extraordinary moment in my life. My daughter's summation of that day was, "This is what divorced families do."

We were all making "the new normal" into our vision for the future.

Remember, you are in the driver's seat of your new life. You can choose whether to get bitter or better. Choosing to be bitter will have lasting negative effects on you and your family. Choosing to be better will enable you and your children to adapt and function in a new way of life, paving the way toward success for all involved. Check yourself for a victim mentality, and if it exists, do the work to change your thought processes into more functional, positive beliefs. Realize that you have been hurt or dealt a cruddy hand. Give yourself compassion, but break free of immobilizing thinking. If your gearshift is stuck, get help learning how to manually shift. You are worth the investment of a professional counselor. To help you get started, here are some steps to self-empowerment:

1. Embrace change: open your mind to new options
2. Movement: start by doing the next right thing
3. Positive thinking: "I can" thinking
4. Own your life: "I get to make my own choices."

5. Welcome Power: "I have the power to choose
    what I want with what I have or can get."
6. Elect a choice: just make a choice
7. Resolve to choose: "I will make a choice today."

As you practice self-empowerment, don't forget to tap into your resources. Look for possible sources of information about single parenting. They could include single friends or family members, a counselor, or a group geared toward single parenting. Groups like DivorceCare and GriefShare may offer ideas for moving forward. Think outside the box. Involve your kids in helping you forge new paths. Get creative with saving and making money. Develop new traditions and memories around birthdays or the holidays.

Resilient Kids

Having a parent stuck in victim mode can handicap children. If children perceive that their parent cannot handle life's difficulties, fear could become a backdrop for their lives. Depending on their age and developmental stage, children could develop over-the-top fearful responses to change throughout their lives.[2] Moving from a victim mindset to one of self-empowerment sends a message to your children that it's okay when life moves on, even if the direction isn't one you chose. It is vitally important to show your kids your ability to adapt and change. If you have been stuck in victim mode, shift your gears out of neutral and into empowerment. Forgive yourself and move into change. Only then can the family begin to function in a healthy fashion.

You can do this! Your brain has the ability to make this shift! God built our brains to change and adapt. Old patterns of thinking can give way to new and healthier patterns. Just think: you can correct potential generations of dysfunction before you. Be the healthy change that your family needs! But, as if changing yourself weren't difficult enough, take a deep breath, because we're about to open the can of worms that is coparenting after divorce.

Dealing with Your Child's Other Parent: Modeling Healthy Relationships with Adults

Self-control is strength. Calmness is mastery. You have to get to a point where your mood doesn't shift based on the insignificant actions of someone else. Don't allow others to control the direction of your life. Don't allow your emotions to overpower your intelligence.

Morgan Freeman

Most parents feel excited about venturing off on a college visit day. Not Tammie. In fact, she dreaded the very thought of it—not because she knew her daughter would soon be moving away, but because her ex-husband would be joining them on the trip. Tammie agonized over the prospect. "He wants to ride in the car with us halfway across the country!" she told me.

She went on to explain that her ex-husband, Gary, was a narcissist, with a gold ribbon in manipulation tactics. She just wasn't ready for a road trip with him. I couldn't have agreed more. I mean, I wouldn't be caught dead enduring a six-hour car ride with someone who can only think about himself and who uses every opportunity to advance his selfish agenda.

"Tammie," I gently probed, "might you have a choice in the matter?"

She retorted quickly, "But it's what my daughter wants."

What a conundrum. Deep down, Tammie knew Gary was a toxic person, but her daughter was still holding on to the dream of having her family back together again. As I worked with Tammie, she realized that her need for emotional safety and stability should take priority over her daughter's unrealistic dream.

So, what happened next? Tammie took a brave step by setting a boundary with Gary, telling him that he couldn't ride in the car with them. This maintained her ability to have self-control.

As predicted, Gary wasn't the least bit happy and tried to gaslight Tammie by saying, "What's the big deal? You should be able to handle this. After all, it is for Megan, and before long she will be gone away from us." (Gaslighting is a manipulation tactic used to manipulate someone into believing they are delusional.)

Gary included just enough truth to make Tammie consider swallowing that gaslight pill. However, she knew better and had healed enough to know that a round trip of twelve hours (plus a weekend) with this schemer would undo a lot of the peace she had worked hard for over the last couple of years. She held to her boundary of separate travel. Gary would no longer have power over her emotions. As Megan adjusted to the idea, Gary entered into victim mode about the unnecessary cost of separate travel. But Tammie held on to her serenity. Later, when she found out that Gary was threatening to bring his girlfriend to the school visit, she talked to Megan about her wishes for the day. Megan protested, "I don't want her to tour with us. It's not her place!"

Tammie requested to Gary that the visit be just the two of them and the children. Luckily, he acquiesced.

The college visit went smoothly, and Tammie felt like she had grown through the experience. "I am learning to navigate this tricky terrain of coparenting with a manipulative master-mind," she told me, "and the best part is, I am gaining mastery over my reactions!"

The Real Picture

Stacey

It would be so easy to write a namby-pamby chapter encouraging readers to collaborate in a partnership to ensure the well-being of their children. But the bulk of this chapter will discuss how to deal with a formidable foe of an ex.

One of those experiences included a dear friend, Marilyn, who found herself sitting in the child support office, waiting for a meeting with her estranged husband and the child support advocate. A TV hanging from the ceiling in the corner of the room blared a video on getting along with a child's other procreator. It rang in her ears as she averted the angry glare of her ex from across the waiting room. She had tried for many years get along with him, but knew that was impossible. She told me one afternoon how she found her power in that situation.

She asked to meet with the child support advocate before her ex-husband arrived. She presented her documentation showing proof of his income, and told them that he would not be transparent about his earnings. She stood up for her emotional safety by requesting that she not be left alone in the room with him. Marilyn thoughtfully told me, "I went back into the waiting room and practiced mindfulness and deep breathing, I ignored the TV—and my ex-husband's death stare—and focused on the goal, which was my children."

When her ex showed up, he did just as Marilyn had predicted: he lied to avoid taking financial responsibility for their children. Marilyn knew if she played the get-along game, she would be chopped liver. She had to be way savvier than that to make sure her kids' needs were met. The child support advocate was now onto her ex, and so Marilyn held onto her peace.

That is a difficult situation to navigate. The key to modeling healthy relationships with adults is first to know who you are dealing with. Of course, this is easier said than done if you have been under the spell of a manipulator for a long time. Here are some indications that you are dealing with a difficult coparenting scenario:

- vindictiveness
- lack of healing
- blame
- shame
- jealousy
- anger
- vengeance
- addiction
- infidelity
- personality disorder

Our advice is to do your homework, understand what you are dealing with, and consult a counselor, if necessary, for an objective opinion. If you determine that the other parent is indeed someone with whom you cannot reason, then you will know how to proceed. Next, you have to learn to control your emotions and reactions to your prior partner. The Serenity Prayer says it best:

> God, grant me the serenity to accept the things
> I cannot change,
> the courage to change the things I can,
> and the wisdom to know the difference.

Sometimes, we have to accept that we cannot make another person rational and fair. Some of us have more difficulty letting that go. Magic happens when we follow the Serenity Prayer and accept what we can't control. We can then change ourselves. Many dynamics surface, and there are many nuances to consider when dealing with a difficult ex. Love and relationships are complicated, impassioned, and fueled with many intense emotions. When a relationship ends, those heightened emotions usually remain. Coparenting then becomes a minefield, with the adults trying to dodge potential explosions. Since many couples had problems cooperating during their marriage, expecting them to do it after going through a traumatic dissolution is often unreasonable.

It is best if you can get along with and work with your child's other parent. Presenting a united front for a child or adolescent is the healthiest option, because, unfortunately, children can and do use discord and lack of communication between their parents as a tool of manipulation. Therefore, it is always a good idea to attempt to keep a line of communication open with the other parent. Even if some of the dynamics listed above exist, it is your responsibility to heal yourself so that you can remain in control of yourself. In doing so, you please God and benefit your children. Know yourself. If you struggle with being a pleaser, then your work will focus on developing strong boundaries. If your tendency is toward pride and self-focus, work on becoming flexible for the sake of your children.

In the remainder of this chapter, let's get practical and discover how we can model healthy relationships with adults— especially for the sake of our kids.

Remove the Emotion

Perhaps, in these conflictual coparenting situations, we can learn from Deborah Serani's advice to employ a more strategic problem-solving model for coparenting.[1] This model focuses on facts instead of emotions. Problems are identified and solutions are generated and negotiated. In this type of problem-solving, there is an exchange of needs and priorities. The focus moves away from either spouse's emotional desires. Think of it as the "Just the facts, ma'am!" approach.

"Jan, it's Billy—he's been in a car accident!" Bob howled to his ex-wife. Later, as they were arguing about Billy's drinking and driving, Bob claimed, "Well, Billy has never been the same since you walked out." Jan retorted, "Well, I'm not dealing with him, I have had way too much to deal with to add this to my plate."

This couple did not employ the strategic model for coparenting. If they had, that conversation might have sounded a bit like this: "Jan, I need to tell you that Billy has been involved in an accident. He is okay, but we need to discuss how to handle the problem."

Jan's response might have been: "I think he needs to receive some treatment. Let me think about whether I can commit to taking him back and forth, and I will get back to you."

In the latter scenario, Bob and Jan removed their emotions from the conversation, dealt with the facts, and worked toward establishing a plan.

Guard against Anger

Why is managing our anger so difficult? Thoughts lead to emotions, which lead to actions, and those actions have consequences. There is no time when our reactivity is tested as much as when we coparent with an ex-spouse. Think about it. There are numerous reasons why coparenting creates volatility. Perhaps you think the other person never loved you, so you feel rejected, which causes you to use anger as a defense against further hurt. That anger has a consequence. So, it's understandable when the Bible guides us to "Be not quick in your spirit to become angry, for anger lodges in the bosom of fools" (Ecclesiastes 7:9). Another anger trigger is what you perceive to be the other coparent's shortcomings in parenting. Nothing makes mama bears roar, or daddy protectors rise up, like perceived damage to their offspring. This is one of the most difficult areas in which to let go. It seems counterintuitive to stay calm when your children encounter things that violate your moral compass. I don't throw this Bible verse at you lightly. Instead, I weep with you as you force yourself to release your death grip of control overprotecting your children. I cuss with you at the audacity of another person who corrupts his own flesh and blood. I gently admonish you to heed the words of Romans 12:19, which, thankfully, starts with an endearing epithet: "Beloved, never avenge yourselves, but leave it to the wrath of God, for it is written, 'Vengeance is mine, I will repay, says the Lord.'"

Oh, how hard this is to let go of potential harm to our children! Where you do have power is to speak truth to your children. John 17:17 says, "Sanctify them in the truth; your word is truth." Although these words refer to God's Truth, which is His Word, I think it is safe to say that if your truth aligns with His Truth, then your children will be covered by protection through the Almighty. And Truth will be the stability that your children search for. I have found God honors that when you exercise self-restraint, and His walls of protection rise up to protect you and your children (Proverbs 25:28).

Empower Your Kids to Advocate for Themselves

Tomasa had a dreadful ex-husband. He was chronically unfaithful to her and lied compulsively. He had been diagnosed with Narcissistic Personality Disorder, and had begun a new marriage that was already marred by conflict. Tomasa fiercely told me about her ex-husband, Lauren:

He is horrible. He doesn't care about the kids. They were with him last weekend and told me about a fight they overheard [between him] and his new wife. The fight went on for hours. Lauren dramatically walked out of the house, demanding the kids get in the car with him when he was in a rage. They were terrified. He then drove around forever! The kids started texting me when this whole thing began. I thought about texting Lauren and demanding that he bring the kids to me. But I stopped and prayed and let go of control. The next text was from the kids saying that they wanted to come home to me. I told them to tell their dad what they wanted, and he said yes and brought them home.

What a turn of events! Tomasa avoided pouring gasoline on a raging fire and prayed for wisdom. Her children learned to use their voices. This wasn't an easy task with a narcissistic father, but she was teaching them to act instead of stepping in and taking care of it for them. Obviously, if your children are in grave danger, there is a time to speak up. Refer to the Serenity Prayer and pray for wisdom to recognize that time. Use the following matrix that Stacey created to see how your coparenting responses change depending on your ability to reason with the other parent. He or she may not change, but you can.

Successful Coparenting Matrix Is it possible to reason with the other parent?	
YES	NO
Be flexible	Let go
Use direct communication (not through kids)	Grieve
Involve each other in all decisions	Pray
Stay focused on kids	Get feelings out elsewhere
Use a businesslike tone	Practice self-control
Show restraint	Set boundaries
Apologize	Get support
Respect each other	Don't react
Compromise	Stay firm

Be aware that your children are watching you. Actions over time create character. They will see your character as you interact with their other parent. They will hear how you talk about and to the other parent. They are witnesses to this race you are running (Hebrews 12:1). Let God help you show your children how to navigate these sometimes-difficult circumstances. Let them witness you maturely handle things that upset you. They will observe your courage and develop strength for themselves. When you show restraint, they will learn self-discipline. As you show tenderness, they become more charitable in their dealings with others.

It might seem like I missed a lot about how to coparent with an easier type of person. Basically, use the Golden Rule: "Do unto others as you would have them do unto you." Use respect, communication, flexibility, and honesty in your dealings. This is a great recipe for all human relationships.

The greatest trouble I see in coparenting concerns emotions. When we struggle with strong emotions, we are unable to access the clarity of mind needed for rational decision-making. This is why I suggest pausing and getting control of your emotions. When you employ God as a help and ask for serenity, you get a sense of peace. Instead of reacting, your thoughts become unclouded, and the thinking brain has the ability to access wisdom and find a solution. Self-control allows room for God to act. Be in control of yourself and your emotions to become a successful team with your coparent.

Take the Good with the Bad

Stacey

One thing I know I can control is choosing to speak truth about our family life. I take plenty of opportunities to talk about good memories with my kids.

I tell them, "Your dad used to love to take you guys out on the boat." Or I share funny stories, like the time that he was eating ham at my mom's house when we were dating. He bit into a whole clove and was so worried about impressing her that he just kept chewing it. We laugh as I describe the look on his face, and how he swallowed that potent spice that was never meant to be ingested. I tell them, "Your dad is a sensitive man."

I describe how he romanced me, and how he felt deeply grieved when his brother died. I recall times when he taught Zach to ride his bike and stopped him just as he was about to slam into a car. Whitney and I get teary-eyed watching old home videos. "He adored you, Whitney," I say through tears.

They then understand why I fell in love with their dad. I also validate their feelings when they struggle with him. Without disparaging him, I tell them, "I get it. I understand how you feel."

I encourage them to use their voices with him, because they are valid. Walk in truth, seek God for guidance, and check yourself before you speak. Go forth and do your best! I did not address one further aspect of dealing with the other coparent, mainly because it deserves a chapter of its own. A big part of this troublesome terrain involves disciplining your children. We will wrestle with this booger of an issue next.

CHAPTER 13

When You're the Bad Guy: Setting Boundaries for Your Child

Daring to set boundaries is about having the courage to love ourselves even when we risk disappointing others.

Brené Brown

"Young lady, what are you doing up at this hour?" Lana shrieked.

It had become a familiar tune playing in the Rhodes home.

Her teenaged daughter, Diedra, snipped back, "Dad doesn't make me go to bed this early ever!"

"It's a school night, and you have that big chemistry test that you know you have to pass in the morning!" Lana insisted.

"You are such a control freak, Mom!" Diedra hissed.

Lana left these interactions filled with anger and frustration that she had to be the "bad guy" parent. She felt like her ex-husband never set any rules for the kids, and this was just one more example of his never considering the outcome of his permissiveness. This situation repeatedly forced Lana to be the heavy in the parenting relationship, leaving her ex as a "Disneyland dad." "All they ever do is fun things with their father," she said. "They don't have rules, bedtimes, or any restrictions. It's as if they are on vacation when they go see him on the weekend. It takes me two days just to get them back in shape, snapping the sass out of them and rehabilitating them back to respecting authority."

Order vs. Chaos

When you are the custodial parent, you can expect to receive the brunt of your children's emotions, as well as their bad behavior. Raising children is a tough job and can be messy at times. Order and structure are essential to a healthy home environment. It is a parent's job to discipline, set boundaries, and reinforce consequences. If this is your legal responsibility, then this part of single parenting may not be particularly fun. It can also be downright frustrating when you feel like your children's other parent is working against you. Kids naturally buck structure. They do this to gain independence, which is a normal developmental phase. However, your job as a parent is to push back and let them know that their buck won't break the fence.

In this chapter, let's roll up our sleeves and explore practical ways of setting those all-important boundaries.

Playground Science

Where do you think kids play on a playground with no fence? Most people would think, "All over the place," or "They ran out into the street," or "They went a thousand different directions." When a study measured children's behavior in such a scenario, the outcomes were not what researchers had anticipated! They discovered that children played in the middle of the unfenced playground and explored their surroundings to a much lesser degree than experts had predicted. Why? The kids were unsure where the limits were. They were reluctant to stray too far from the caregiver, remaining dependent on the caregiver for assurance. So, when placed in a fenced-in playground, where did the kids go? Right up to the fence. They pushed to the limit because they felt more at ease to explore the space. They ran with abandon and played with a sense of security.

This study suggests that boundaries and limits are good. They help our children develop autonomy within a safe space while they are still at home under a roof of protection and loving guidance. It is a parent's job to keep structure in the home. Regular routines, including chores, provide consistency and help develop self-discipline. When children begin to understand the requirements and rules within their family, they begin gaining competence at completing daily tasks. In turn, they develop independence, which boosts self-esteem.

Our go-to authorities on boundaries are who we affectionately call "The Boundaries Guys": John Townsend and Henry Cloud. In their book *Boundaries with Kids,* they sum up the idea of boundaries this way: "Give freedom, require responsibility, render consequences, and be loving throughout."[1] These guys get it right on so many parenting fronts: teaching children to recognize danger and seek safety, showing them how to make better choices so they can reap the rewards, and demonstrating how good choices bring life, not death. The authors validate our children's hatred of the boundaries when they protest them, and then cheer us on to continue to enforce them in spite of the pushback. Best of all, they show parents how to understand and empathize with our offspring about how hard it is to obey. As a parent, you provide the guardrails surrounding your children's upbringing. Reward exceptional performance or achievement of a new skill, but do not make rewarding habits or routines part of children's daily expectations. All of these suggestions are valuable as you navigate single parenting and boundary setting.

It Is for Your Good

There is plenty in God's Word about His discipline of us. His discipline mirrors what we should do with our children. He gives us a book with instructions for the best possible life. The Bible is full of guidelines, limits, and warnings about the dangers and pitfalls we face. Yet He gives us freedom to go out on our own and try it our own way. Inevitably, after failure, we come crawling back and are received with grace. The consequences we encounter urge us to learn from our bad behavior and not repeat it. This is the way we learn to have a good life. We are encouraged to raise our children in the same way.

From the Old Testament to the New Testament, parents are charged with teaching children the right way to live, forming children to obey that teaching, and cultivating respect for parents (Proverbs 22:6, Ephesians 6:1, Exodus 20:12). As a single parent, you can model holding to this responsibility regardless of what the other parent is doing. Raising your children by these standards gives them the best possible chance for success in the world. As they learn what their life duties are, they will fulfill the edict to "carry their own load" (Galatians 6:5). Don't you think we could use a generation of load-carriers?

Jen's Story

At fifteen, Eric was hell on wheels, disrespecting everything and everyone around him. His single mother, Jen, was too overwhelmed to ever tell him no. Eric truly believed that he was entitled to whatever he wanted, whenever he wanted it, at any cost. Beaten down by the betrayal of Eric's dad, Jen wasn't able to find her power as a disciplinarian. Eric learned that his toddler fits, which turned into childhood defiance and then teenage opposition, were the key to his power to get his way. It worked for him, and his lack of boundaries created a monster that was a lot harder to tame than the youngster who threw himself into a convulsing tantrum on the mini-mart floor. This poor boy was set on a path to the slammer, all because of the absence of boundaries.

Think about limits and guidelines in your home. Which areas feel out of control? Which areas do you fear? In which areas do you need guidance and advice? Take your time, talk it out with a trusted person, and make a plan. Here are some areas for you to consider setting boundaries.

1. Bedtimes: Set age-appropriate bedtimes for your kids and stick to them. Weekend bedtimes can be later, but not too late, as this prevents the body from settling into a normal circadian rhythm.

2. Chores: Let the kids help with this one. Write down all that has to be done and let them pick. If they can't agree, then assign them.

3. Manners: You decide whether slang is okay, and whether you want to hear "yes ma'am" and "yes sir," "please" and "thank you" from your little darlings.

4. Electronics: Set time limits for video games. Program phones to shut off texting and calling at certain times. There's an app for that! Or make them charge them in the kitchen at night. Also think about limits set on phones at mealtimes.

5. Friends: Require that you meet friends that they will be driving with. Call parents before your child goes over to their house to play with their kids.

6. Sex: Set expectations on premarital sex and/or birth control. Be upfront about the risks of

unmarried sex, like STIs, unintended pregnancies, and subsequent emotional issues. Decide if you will allow teens to be in their rooms with the doors shut with boy/girlfriends.

7. Drugs and Alcohol: Will you allow underage drinking in your home? What will you do if you catch them with it in their possession or catch them under the influence?

8. Eating: Set the tone for healthy eating in your home. Set boundaries about eating outside the kitchen, hoarding food, or making messes.

9. Freedoms: As they grow older, maybe they get the privilege of uninterrupted time alone in their room. Maybe they decide their own curfew as they show trustworthiness. Maybe you let them pick out their own clothes as they enter the teen years.

Remember: Limits = A Sense of Security

When kids experience your limits, they feel secure. They develop character, self-discipline, and the ability to accept "no."

They are more able to respect authority, more pleasant to be around, and are better able to foster healthy relationships. Limits will have a lasting impact on their social, career, and financial lives. They will learn to be good stewards of their freedom!

Even if you have to be the bad guy, do it, because the bad guy later becomes the hero. As you watch your children grow into healthy, responsible adults, you will reap the rewards. Don't agree to the "buy now, pay later" scheme of ignoring boundaries for the sake of peace in your home. If you sow disrespect and refusal now, you will reap a harvest of maladjusted adolescents who will wreak havoc on your future peace. Those little beings are a lot easier to pilot when they are young than when they are older and have been allowed to taste the freedoms of rebellion and power. You may temporarily become the unfavorite parent, but you will find that when your children seek safety, they will run into your boundary-loving arms! Teach them to hear "no." Train them to communicate with you. Reward them for good behavior. Discipline the behavior that will hurt them or others in the future. Teach them gratitude and how to work hard. Give them the structure they crave. Be the parent that creates predictability, and therefore safe ground for their souls.

Rugrats Aren't So Bad, Either

Stacey

I love it when my kids laugh and rib me, saying, "You were so strict you didn't even let us watch *Rugrats*. What's up with that, Mom?"

I tell them, just like I did when they were little, that I wanted to teach them to honor each other, and that particular cartoon didn't seem to exude that value. They tease me when they remind me that I nixed Mature-rated video games with vile language and disregard for the law. We laugh at those trying times. But I raised two very well-mannered adults. I'd like to think they are thankful for that! You, too, can partner with God to set and enforce good boundaries that will create stellar human beings.

Perk alert! As your children learn respect for themselves and others, it frees you up to have a life of your own. Now that your children understand that you are an actual person with rights, desires, and hopes, you might be able to dream about dating. Read on to find out if you are ready!

CHAPTER 14

Am I Ready?: Dating as a Single Parent

Dating for two is difficult; dating in a crowd is downright complicated.

FamilyLife

ating. Sometimes we get it right. Sometimes we crash and
burn. I have been optimistic, but also a true Debbie
Downer at the thought of going out.

Dating is hard. I wrote this when we were nine months
into the COVID pandemic, which put a real damper on social-
izing. (As if dating weren't hard enough already.) I always liken
the dating ordeal to an intake session in my counseling office.
It kicks off with a seemingly endless set of questions: "How
old are you? How many kids do you have? How is your relationship with them? Tell me about why you are single. How
has it been for you? Any mental health issues? Crazy exes?
What brings you here today? What are your goals?"

The only difference with dating is that I can't take notes! That, and maybe there's a little less formality and a whole lot more "slyness" in dating. It is helpful if you look at dating as a learning process. With each date, you learn something new about yourself and the world around you.

Navigating a Strange New World

Dating can plunge new singles into a strange new world. They've been down this road before, yet here they are again—reliving old insecurities and dating jitters, navigating awkward circumstances. And as two strangers connect, they start to determine if they enjoy each other's company, if they have similar interests and values, and if they have chemistry. Perhaps one of the biggest obstacles to overcome is scheduling a date when you don't have your kids. If you are dating another single parent and they are on the standard visitation schedule, it's a good chance that you have your children on the opposite weekends.

Dating takes time, energy, and emotion. After becoming single, it comes with plenty of challenges. But with some guidelines, it can be navigated well. In this chapter, we'll explore some best dating practices, the impact your dating can have on your kids, and some unique circumstances single parents must consider. Let's begin with questions you should ask yourself to see if you are ready to date:

Do I have the time?

Do I have the energy?

Do I have the emotional capacity?

One way to look at this is from the other side. Put yourself on the receiving side of things. If your dating partner were too busy to make time for you, how would you feel? Ask yourself, "Do I truly have the time for a relationship?" Sometimes it's hard to tell if your potential date is lacking energy or emotion. You will find that out over time. One unfortunate way to find that out is when you express interest, and then get ghosted. (We know what that feels like.) For heaven's sake, don't be the one making your suitor guess why you didn't respond!

Emotional capacity is where most newly single folks miss the bus. They have not done the grieving work that we discussed in chapter 3. Make sure that you are healing from past hurts before you begin a new relationship. Otherwise, you'll bring in what is called baggage. Having an ex-husband or wife doesn't have to mean baggage. Being a widow or widower doesn't have to cause suitors to bring out the luggage rack. And choosing to have a child alone does not necessarily mean you are lugging carry-ons. Do your work to make sure you don't have anger, bitterness, depression, or other attachments that you haven't processed. We will always carry pockets of pain from prior situations, but make sure they have been discussed and fixed prior to signing up for match.com. Be sure that you have given yourself enough time after a breakup to begin dating. Frequently, people spin around and quickly enter into another relationship to avoid the uncomfortable feelings of loneliness, sorrow, and fear. That equals the need for a separate freight car to carry your parcels. If you date too early, you will stress out yourself, your date, and your kids.

Best Practices for Dating

A Christian organization called FamilyLife, an offshoot of Campus Crusade for Christ (now called Cru), was founded back in the 1970s to help families raise children in a healthy Christian manner. They cite eleven best practices for dating as a single parent, emphasizing that, in dating, competing attachments form when the partners have children at home. Spending time with one means that the others are "left waiting . . . and wondering how their relationship with you is being influenced by your relationship with the other."[1] Children can become insecure when this happens. Being aware of this can lead to healthy discussions with your children and potential date. FamilyLife suggests having pre-dating conversations with your children to assess how they feel about your dating. It makes them feel that they are truly part of the process. While they don't get to make all the decisions about your future, including them will help them feel respected and included. You should also give older children a chance to go at their own pace with regard to meeting and spending time with your partner. Be aware of their fears and help your children work through them. You will learn in chapter 17 how to listen and validate your children in this area, which will make them feel more secure.

When broaching the subject of dating with your children, author Margot Starbuck stresses in her book, *The Grown Woman's Guide to Online Dating*, that the focus should be on your kids and less on you.[2] She says it's essential that parents base the amount of information they give their kids about their social life on the kids' ages. "Smalls (ages 0–12) have no need to know; Mediums (ages 13–18) need to know when they need to know, and Bigs (age 18 and up) need to know before they need to know." If you run the risk of running into your kids while you're out on a date, it's a good idea that they know you are seeing someone. Your kids are egocentric from ages three to seven, meaning that they are unable to see the world from another person's point of view. Sounds a lot like your teenager, too, huh? David Elkind coined the term adolescent egocentrism[3] to describe the same phenomenon as the early stage described above. Bottom line: Your kids primarily care about what you are doing if it affects them. So, address it when it is in *their* best interest to do so.

Put God First

We understand that it is not easy to be alone. God knows that. It is normal to want another person to partner with and help with the children. To have a life partner to love and cherish you is a great gift from the Lord. It is difficult to put what we think will bring happiness on the back burner and seek God first (Matthew 6:33–34), but the promise is that God knows what we need better than us, and He will provide what's best.

As we work to surrender the want for relationship and focus on our job as parents, God can have the space to work. We are encouraged not to exasperate or embitter our children (Colossians 3:21, Ephesians 6:4). And if we put ourselves first without thinking about our dating readiness, we can do just that. God is the God of order and serenity. When we follow His plans, our lives tend to go smoothly. So often, we jump onto our own roads to happiness without remembering to consult Him, and those roads end up going nowhere! The good news is, God gives do-overs, and is ready and waiting to offer up His grace when we get ahead of Him!

Protect the Little Ones

Babs flew into my office in a rage.

"Billy says that he has a new family! He told me that his dad told him, 'You are going to have a new sibling soon!' I am so cotton-picking angry that Pete dropped this bomb on Billy. What the heck was he thinking?"

Pete, Babs's ex-husband, had hardly let the ink dry on the divorce papers. (He may not have even had them drafted when he began the relationship with Karen.) Now, Babs's two sons were spending time with Karen and had noticed that her stomach appeared to be growing daily. Her boys had so many questions that she asked me for the number of a child therapist to help them adjust to a life from which she had tried to protect them. This is an example of a parent's relationship choices affecting the child. We know that little Billy is in an egocentric stage, so having more siblings around will surely affect his rank in the household. Babs raised him in a Christian home where he learned that babies come from the love of a husband and wife who are married, so he was confused as to why Daddy lives with his friend, why she is having a baby, and why the baby will be his sibling. This father did not protect or nurture his son from truths that were too big for him to bear so early.

Dating Self-Assessment

This is a self-assessment to help you determine your readiness to date. Take a paper and pen—or better yet, your trusty journal—and answer the following questions earnestly and honestly. Noodle around on some of these questions; really dig deeply to gauge your preparedness for courtship.

- Am I ready to date?
- Do I need to have a relationship to feel whole?
- Do I have the time to devote to a significant other?
- Have I processed my emotions about difficulties in my life?
- Do I have the energy to give a new relationship while also giving to my children?
- Have I talked to God about it? What does He say?
- What did I learn from prior relationships?
- Are my children stable?
- Are their needs met?
- Are my needs met?
- Am I being selfish?

Red Flags

When you take these questions into account, decide that the time is right for dating, and dip your toe into the dating pool, you still need to analyze your date's suitability. Read over the following items and check your date on each item. When you see red flags, proceed with caution. It is really best to turn around and run the other way if you see more than one of these in a potential partner.

- Incessant talk about the ex
- Idealizing you or others (as evidenced by referring to people as perfect)
- Being a man/woman hater
- Not returning calls
- Ghosting others
- Moving too quickly

Little Eyes Watching

Consider what messages your dating sends to your children. They learn that their needs can be met while you are taking time for yourself. They learn that life goes on after heartbreak, tragedy, and loss. You are teaching them resiliency, the ability to bounce back from life's blows. They see your courage as you go through the gauntlet of choosing, rejecting, and being rejected. You model rebounding and flexibility. As we discussed above, you don't share every detail with them, but they will see you and ask questions. They are learning and mentally taking notes all the time. When Sally watches her mom text a love interest and then the conversation stops, she learns to not idealize every interaction with a boy. Maybe Sally doesn't know the exact content of the inappropriate texts that her mom was receiving or the detailed reasons that she cut it off, but she begins to understand that she must be wise in relationships. When Wade watches his father treat the women he takes out with respect and courtesy, he develops chivalry. He learns how to treat a young lady with kindness. Use the time with your kids while they're young to model healthy behavior. If you blow it, admit it, and talk to them about what you have learned. When you model authenticity, you make it okay to make mistakes and admit them to one another.

In summary, be intentional about dating. Ask yourself the serious questions above before you sign up to start swiping left and right. Run your ideas by a trusted wise friend or therapist and get their thoughts. Meet with God and check for His stamp of approval. Do a gut check and make sure you have peace about the process before you begin. When you do, make sure you check in with yourself and others to make sure you are seeing the situation objectively. Also, check in with your kids and allow them to ask questions at their level and pace. Remember to keep the focus on them, not yourself, when deciding what information to share.

Perhaps there is no bigger step to take in the process of single parenting than deciding to date. That's good, because it means that you have done your work. Whatever reason you are single has not kept you from risking again. If done properly, it means that you are willing to risk vulnerability and rejection. Here's what C. S. Lewis wrote about love and relationships:

> To love at all is to be vulnerable. Love anything and your heart will be wrung and possibly broken. If you want to make sure of keeping it intact you must give it to no one, not even an animal. Wrap it carefully round with hobbies and little luxuries; avoid all entanglements. Lock it up safe in the casket or coffin of your selfishness. But in that casket, safe, dark, motionless, airless, it will change. It will not be broken; it will become unbreakable, impenetrable, irredeemable. To love is to be vulnerable.[4]

Enjoy the exhilarating ride of finding love, perhaps for the first time. Who knows? Perhaps you could be creating your own Brady Bunch!

Next, we will move into a discussion of life-giving practices like cultivating gratitude, holding space for your children, and accepting your imperfection. You are learning all the ingredients to become a successful single parent. Next, be prepared to be challenged in a new way as you create new healthy routines for yourself and your children.

CHAPTER 15

Attitude of Gratitude: Choosing Thankfulness

What if today we were grateful for everything?

Charlie Brown

If there were ever a real Eeyore on the face of this planet, it would be Richard. He was the epitome of the gloomy donkey in the *Winnie the Pooh* books. Richard was only capable of seeing the glass half-empty. I am a glass-half-full person, and honestly, I have difficulty with negative people.

"I don't like people!" Richard proudly told me one day. My problem? I am so positive that I don't take that comment at face value and believe it . . . but that is a subject for another book. Anyway, I retorted to Richard, "Seriously, you seem like a really kind person. Do you really hate people?"

"Yes," Richard admitted. "I am a cynic."

He believed that people only wanted to take something from him. He described his relationship with his daughter:

"She only calls me if she needs something. Forget that! I will not be used."

Had Richard borrowed just one drop of my optimism, he might have seen that his daughter's needs could be the catalyst for forging a deeper relationship with her. It is tragic that connections with his children remain shallow because of his detrimental view.

Richard was a brilliant businessman and had a rich bank of experiences in his field. His wisdom can be an incredible resource for others. People often beseech him for guidance in his trade. Richard's standard answer to them is, "I charge $1,000 an hour."

He claimed that it would be a waste of his valuable time to help others. Interestingly, most of that valuable time is spent at home by himself. I finally began to believe Richard was really who he said he was, and I vowed to keep praying for him.

Around Christmastime, he called me with a story he just "had to tell me." He was in a Goodwill store and was standing in line waiting to check out. He had told me the week before that he would be alone on Christmas and that he was just going to forget that it was even a holiday. The holidays had been difficult for him since his mother died, and that year, his children wouldn't be coming due to the COVID pandemic. However, the kids had found a way to come home and visit their single dad. When Richard found out he would have visitors, he began thinking about how to bring a little holiday festivity into his home (the Grinch tree that I had bought him didn't quite complete the look). That day in the thrift store, he commented to the elderly lady in line in front of him that the decorative bowl she was about to purchase would be perfect in his formal dining room. He asked her, "Are there any more back there like that?" She said, "No, I didn't notice any."

After she checked out, she turned around and handed the bowl to Richard. When he resisted the gift, she told him, "Accept this blessing." He stood there admiring it for a moment, and before he could thank her, she was gone. The checkout lady told him that she comes to shop at the Goodwill store every day and seems to be a "nice old lady."

His text to me said, "What is wrong with me? I had goosebumps and almost started crying."

I responded, "Not a thing. That is beautiful!"

He agreed and said that he just wanted to share his praise story with me. He then texted a picture labeled, "A $3 miracle bowl!" I really hope that this is the beginning of Richard's shift toward gratitude and positivity; his tears and goosebumps indicate that God just may be involved in making that happen.

The Practice of Gratitude

I love the work of Ann Voskamp. In her book *One Thousand Gifts*, she eloquently describes the small gifts present in our everyday lives. During my difficult separation and divorce, I couldn't put down her book. Ann's voluminous verbiage kindled a fire inside me to write. I opened my eyes and began seeing the little things around me that I was grateful for: The steam from my cup of coffee wafting in the morning air; my warm, cozy blanket on a cold, crisp morning; the hum of the air conditioning singing in the summer night; the hint of vanilla from the candle in the next room. I began to document the prism-like dew dancing on my windshield, and the streams of sun shining through the glistening leaves of my backyard mulberry tree. My journaling turned into a daily gratitude list that seemed luscious with descriptions that made me glad in my surroundings.

This simple act during a dark time clouded by loss, loneliness, and confusion was enough to keep my head above water. I began to focus on the here and now, and not project my fears into the future. As I engaged in mindfulness and gave thanks for each thing, I blocked my mind from reliving traumatizing memories that used to depress me. Gratitude became a lifeline for me.

While it might feel like a stretch to some, Ann writes that "the secret to joy is to keep seeking God where we doubt He is."[1] When I did this, I found Him everywhere! I began to see His blessings all over! Her concept of thankfulness centers on the word *eucharisteo*. It means to give thanks. She explains, "Because remembering with thanks is what causes us to trust; to really believe. Remembering, giving thanks, is what makes us a member again of the body of Christ. Remembering, giving thanks, is what puts us back together again in this hurried, broken, fragmented world."[2]

Finding gratitude is an essential step in recovery programs. Having an attitude of gratitude switches our focus from problems to blessings. We all know people who never seem to have problems. When you ask them how they are, some piously pop off with, "I'm blessed." This can rub me the wrong way when I hear it because it seems inauthentic. I would rather hear someone lament and curse honestly over their situation, and then turn in faith and notice the good things God has blessed them with. This is not the same as being a pessimist. Pessimists stay stuck in the negative, never attempting to see the good things in life.

A Thankful Body

Stephen

I recommend the best way to increase your well-being and improve your body's physical and emotional health: find thankfulness, just as Stacey described. The body-brain connection is crucial for health. Fostering an attitude of gratitude creates new neural connections in the pleasure center of the brain. Gratitude increases the positive neurochemicals dopamine and serotonin. These are known to reduce stress and increase feelings of well-being.[3] This, in turn, lowers the stress hormone cortisol—the one which contributes to fear and anxiety. Amazing, isn't it? Gratitude boosts our mood and actually makes us feel happier! The hypothalamus regulates our sleep, among other things. Psychiatric counselor M. R. Chowdhury says that "receiving and displaying simple acts of kindness activates the hypothalamus," resulting in better sleep.[4] When we sleep better, we wake up more positive, energized, and ready to start our day. So much happens when we sleep. Our memories from the day are consolidated into longer-term storage, making room for new memories. Healthy sleep helps our immune system fight disease. If the brain isn't healthy, the body will suffer. Our thoughts really do affect our physical well-being!

The Psalmist's Lament

We love the Psalms because they are so human. David's lament as he pours out his difficulty feels so familiar to us. We can feel his torment as he bares his emotions in so many of the Psalms. We are validated in our anguish as we review this spiritual giant's strong negative feelings. They mimic my bleeding heart as it was penned on the pages of my journal during the decline of my marriage. The best part for me, however, is when the torrent begins to subside and the verbiage changes to that of gratitude. For instance, Psalm 116:10 (NLT) says, "In my discouragement, I thought, they are lying when they say I will recover." But, in verse 16, the sentiment switches to "O Lord. You have freed me from my bonds and I will serve you forever." There is so much hope in the reversal of your stream of consciousness. We would do well to follow the example of the Psalmist, turning to praise after we bemoan our difficulties.

The Balm of Journaling

Stacey

I recommend that my clients purchase and use a red journal to write down their anger. (We often associate the color red with anger.) Ginger was a betrayed wife, and the torment of many years of infidelity was locked up in her soul like a caged animal. I knew that she had to begin to get in touch with the anger in order to heal. So, I told her to rant like crazy in her red anger journal and get the feelings out on a daily basis. As Ginger began to scrawl on the pages of that red book, the venom began seeping out of her traumatized body and onto the pages, allowing her to release her tears. "I cannot see anything but crimson! It's like I am stuck in rage!" Ginger screeched. I thanked her for reminding me of the other part of the assignment. I told her, "Grab another journal and begin to make a gratitude list. Start by writing out the small things that you are thankful for each day." After a few weeks of compliance, Ginger reported to me, "I feel more balanced now, like the bad isn't pent up or spewing all over him or others. It's like I have a sense that the bad things happened in the past, but good things are happening now, too. I can move forward." Ginger learned a valuable lesson that day. Awareness and recognition of present good aided her in healing from a horrific history.

Are you wondering where you stack up in the area of gratitude? Are you a grateful person? If you tend toward negative thinking, it's never too late to turn your thinking around. Gratitude is a skill you can cultivate. Remember, you can retrain your brain from negative thinking to positive thinking. There is always something to be grateful for. Here's an exercise to get you started:

Looking around me now, I see_____, and I am grateful for it because_____.

Today, I thank God for _____.

Commit to spending five minutes a day for the next thirty days listing things you are grateful for. Watch your gratitude meter grow!

The Entitlement Fix

Modeling an attitude of gratitude greatly benefits your children. Gratitude is the single greatest defense against a rising epidemic among our nation's kids and young adults: entitlement. (It's been around for more than a decade, and some experts suggest we are living in the Age of Entitlement.)[5] Perhaps nothing frustrates parents more than experiencing their own offspring being expectant and ungrateful. Teach your children to write thank-you notes expressing gratitude.

While these may seem like a thing of the past, they teach your kids to slow down, take a moment to recognize kindness, and appropriately express gratitude. Even if it is just an email or text, teaching them to recognize kindness and to convey thanks to others creates a bridge of communication and a circle of connection with others. If your children can learn this, it will greatly impact the way they interact with others. Your offspring will also benefit from the same positive effects on their brains and bodies.

We know we must appropriately process and express emotions to heal from the trauma of divorce. Incorporating an appreciative spirit is essential. It gives us a hopeful attitude. Whether you are a Spencer Sunshine or a Debbie Downer, remember that an attitude of thanksgiving switches perspective from hopeLESS to hopeFUL! Just like turning the rudder of a ship, you can turn your negative experiences into belief in better times to come.

As you begin to cultivate this newfound grace-filled life, you will find that you have more room to be there for your children. Read on as we address the most beautiful way to be "with" your kids.

CHAPTER 16

Holding Space

When little people are overwhelmed by big emotions,
it's our job to share our calm, not join their chaos.

L. R. Knost

Ashley marched into the kitchen and slammed her books on the counter.

"I am done with Mrs. Wilson! I am just over it!"

Ashley's dad would not tolerate such disrespect of elders, especially Ashley's teacher.

"No, ma'am!" huffed Ed. "You know better than to make such a fuss. You need to get ahold of yourself and your emotions. Now, pick up those books and go straight to your room and figure out what you did to make Mrs. Wilson so upset with you."

Frustrated, but knowing that there was no reasoning with her dad, Ashley grabbed her books and marched up the stairs.

There, now that's better, Ed thought to himself. *A peaceful home, that's what I'm talking about.*

What Ashley's father didn't realize is that she needed to be heard. When he sent his daughter up to her room, Ashley needed work out whatever issue she had with Mrs. Wilson on her own. She did not have the benefit of her father's wisdom or experience, because he shut her down before she could talk about the problem. Ed had strict rules about running the household, and those took precedence over creating a relationship. He refused to hear Ashley out because he feared that he would lose control of his household.

Rules over Relationship = Rebellion and Repression

Ed missed a valuable opportunity to speak into his daughter's life. Ashley did not feel heard by her father. When we refuse to hear our kids out, their unconscious response can be *I will never be angry, because if I do, I will lose love from others.* When this scenario occurred time and time again, Ashley began to believe that her voice didn't matter, and she stopped trusting the angry feelings that arose from within when she was treated unfairly.

Another single parent, Melissa, fearfully raised her daughter, Jaida. Jaida paraded in one mid-April day, waving her cell phone and proudly showing her mom the latest mini prom dress she just "had to have!"

Melissa retorted with, "I'll smack you into next year if you even think about looking at that kind of hoochy-mama dress!" Thank goodness, she resisted the urge to say, "Only sluts wear that kind of dress."

Jaida retreated to her room and made a grand plan to get that exact dress and hide it from her mom. She did just that, wearing the mother-approved dress as she left on prom night, then promptly changing into the skimpy one that defied her mom and celebrated her independence.

Neither the response of Ashley's father nor that of Jaida's mother left either child ready to face the world securely. Ashley became withdrawn and compliant; Jaida became rebellious. They each developed a negative coping skill to deal with parents who failed to recognize and validate their feelings. Imagine if Melissa had calmly sat with Jaida and talked with her about the dress, and maybe even had gone to the store with her to try it on. I wonder if Jaida's own insecurities would have surfaced without the aid of her mom's judgment. Even if they didn't, a validating approach could have avoided a battle between the two. Listening and understanding doesn't mean that you give up your right to make parenting decisions. Melissa still has veto power and can gently tell Jaida that, as much as she loves the dress, she is not willing to buy one for her that exposes so much of her body.

Holding Space

Both Ed and Melissa needed to learn how to listen to their kids, hold space for their children, and validate their feelings. What does "holding space" mean? Because of its therapeutic potential, this idea has grown in popularity among therapists, mental health coaches, and other counselors in the last few years. It is an act of love in which the hearer patiently listens as the other person expresses feelings, processes pain, and works through the issue. It is a sacred space where the speaker feels accepted and not judged. Where emotions are not only accepted, but encouraged. It is a place to vent without being "fixed." And when listeners succeed at holding space, something very special can happen: the speaker, feeling loved and supported, can grow by this simple, respectful act.

When holding space, the listener practices selflessness. It is not about the listener, but the speaker. This is not the time to give advice, or to feel important, or to lead and guide. It is simply time to be with the other person. There is no expectation and no pretense in holding space. In its truest form, holding space allows those speaking to open their souls and come out of hiding. This process lays the groundwork for being fully known by another human being. This builds the basis for intimacy. What a precious thing to give our children: a place to be seen, heard, and accepted.

The benefit to getting this one right is big, as is the cost of getting it wrong. If you hold space correctly, your children will feel strong and supported, and will have the best chance of being emotionally healthy. But when holding space is overlooked or done poorly, you can expect kids who rebel or develop various mental illnesses, poor coping skills, and bad relationship choices.

Validation

Stacey

What many parents find most challenging about holding space is the act of "validating." They confuse validating a child's experience with endorsing behavior. But we encourage parents to validate, even when they disagree. For me, when my daughter announced that she was going to dye her hair blue, my insides were saying, "Oh no, not blue! My beautiful, brown-haired baby girl will not have blue hair." Instead of reacting to my inner thoughts, I put myself aside. I listened and questioned. I found out a lot about my daughter. She likes to be different. She finds satisfaction in being an individual and expressing herself in the way she wants to. As I listened to her, she felt like I was accepting her, whether I liked blue hair or not. Granted, she was nineteen years old, but I could have really damaged our relationship if I didn't listen and validate her experience. In fact, she would have dyed her hair blue anyway. The truth is, she looked cute as a button with her blue hair . . . and her purple hair . . . and her green hair! She is beautiful no matter what color her hair is, and I lived through it all! Your children may be young, meaning you have more authority to guide them. In this case, validation still works, but you gently say no in the end. It sounds like this: "Billy, I know you want to play that video game longer. I see that you are really excited that you made it to that level, but you agreed to the rule to shut it off at 8 p.m." When you validate the experience and feelings behind what a child is saying, you have earned the right to be heard. Then, you are open to ask questions like, "Do you see any downsides?" or "Have you thought about how you might feel in the future?"

One of the most difficult subjects that parents will discuss with their children is sexuality. Avoiding the conversation because it makes you uncomfortable does not serve your children. A full discussion of how to have this important conversation is outside the scope of this book. But this is important to emphasize: you need to validate that receiving attention from an admirer, as well as experiencing sexual stimulation and affection, all feel very good. If you don't validate normal human desire in your teens because you've ignored or demonized it, then the first time they experience this, they will feel duped by you! Parents fail to validate because of fear. You might be afraid to have the tough conversations. You might fear that your children will equate validation with approval. But when you are able to listen and seek understanding, even when you disagree, you can help your children navigate difficult decisions and situations they will face. You love and serve your kids well by helping them think through situations they're likely to face—before they happen! Then your kids are more likely to listen to your advice.

Although we may want to deny it, our children move toward independence the day they leave the womb. This is how God planned it to be. When they start bucking at the gate to get out, see it as a sign of maturity and safety, rather than a threat to you. They are showing readiness to conquer the world on their own. You know they are not totally ready, but don't take offense. Welcome these movements toward growth instead, and be there when they fall, rather than wait until they are out of your sight and have to learn it by themselves.

When children and teens feel validated, they gain developmental skills that build self-confidence.[1] "They learn how to correctly label and communicate how they feel," explains therapist Laura Braziel. "They learn how to tolerate intense emotions and self-soothe. They learn to problem-solve rather than stuff their feelings. And they learn to trust themselves rather than look to others to tell them how to feel and be."[2] As a therapist who counsels teens and parents, Braziel believes that, along with the skills of listening, balance, and support, validation provides the positive parenting that kids need to feel valued and respected.[3]

Validation doesn't mean that parents fail to offer boundaries. Relationships without rules result in chaos. We know that firm expectations and boundaries are essential in running a home, but boundaries must include acceptance and validation. Further, listening and understanding do not replace natural consequences. You love your child by enforcing the rules you've established for your home. But you help your child deal with the results of their actions as an understanding ally rather than a harsh taskmaster.

God has appointed you captain of this parenting ship, and He wants you to guide this boat safely and calmly. Biblical support is found in James 1:19, which says, "My dear brothers and sisters, take note of this: Everyone should be quick to listen, slow to speak and slow to become angry" (NIV). In your home, in your family, you are the boss! Believe that you can do it! The things that kids bring home could shift your boat off course if you aren't prepared for them. These loaded moments could be anything from, "Mom, I am failing math," to "Dad, I am pregnant." If you are grounded in the fruits of the Spirit, self-control will help you manage your inner thoughts, often helping you keep them to yourself so that you can hold space for your child's feelings, thoughts, and opinions. Practicing patience with hair colors, language, behaviors, and differing ideas will help you model emotional regulation for your children. Exude love and kindness to your children, and if you can't, pray for God to grant it to you!

When We Hold Space

During the flooding in Houston after Hurricane Harvey, many children became traumatized. Little Billy was no different. Jim and Cyndi felt like they had done a good job of helping their children in the aftermath of the storm. Jim carried Billy out of the house on his shoulders in the dark of night as their home was inundated with water. As they trudged through the floodwaters into safety, the couple knew that this incident would have lasting impacts on all their lives. Three years later, Hurricane Laura was threatening the Gulf Coast once again. Jim had talked with Billy every time there was a thunderstorm, listening to his concerns. But now, Billy's fear was taking over.

The little boy said, "I'm okay with thunder and rain, but I just don't want to have to swim!"

It would have been easy for Jim to simply tell Billy that he would likely not have to swim, but instead, he listened and asked Billy questions.

"Tell me about that, Billy," Jim said while holding space.

"Well, the water is gross, not like pool water, and it would be dark, and I can't see in the dark," Billy said anxiously.

"Okay, so you don't like swimming in nasty flood waters in the dark, right?" said Jim, parroting Billy.

"Yes, I don't want to swim out of the house!"

Jim responded with understanding. "Well, Billy, that makes a lot of sense, and I don't want to swim out, either. What do you say we blow up your *Jaws* float just in case it floods again, and you can ride out on that if it happens again?"

Billy smiled, hugged his dad, and felt safe and secure in the midst of the frightening circumstances. Billy felt ready to weather the storm because of Jim's ability to listen to his son.

You may be wondering what types of things to say while you are holding space for your kids. Open-ended questions are best. Your goal can be to encourage them to talk more. Below are some tools for your parenting journey.

Talking Tools

- Stop what you're doing
- Make eye contact
- Physically lean in
- "Tell me more . . ."
- "What else?"
- Ask general questions

Open-Ended Questions

- "What would you do if . . . ?"
- "How would you feel if . . . ?"
- "Have you thought about . . . ?"

After they begin talking, use statements that indicate that you are listening and that you believe what they are saying is valid. Try some of the suggestions below.

Validating Statements

- "I see how that might be true."
- "That makes sense."
- "You are really feeling_____" (repeating what they've named)
- "I see you are upset."
- "Hmmm . . . "
- "Let me think about that."
- "I see you care a lot about that."
- "You might be right."

Can you hear how avoiding the kinds of conversation-stoppers that Melissa's father and Jaida's mother used keeps the lines of communication between you and your children open?

What Your Children Need from You

Stephen

As Stacey and I counsel folks, we often begin by giving them a questionnaire asking how they felt about their parents growing up. We inquire how often their parents demonstrated qualities like kindness, joy, and forgiveness, and how often they

demonstrated qualities like anger, disapproval, and unpredict-
ability. As you might imagine, the results are telling![4]

Now, switch this exercise around, seeing yourself through
your children's eyes so that you can become aware of how your
relational skills could be affecting them. Rate yourself on these
qualities to see how you might measure up in your child's eyes.
Answer them with Always, Very Often, Sometimes, Hardly
Ever, Never:

gentle
stern
loving
disapproving
distant
close/intimate
kind
angry
demanding
caring
harsh
trustworthy
joyful
forgiving
good

cherished me

impatient

unreasonable

strong

protective

passive

encouraging

unpredictable

Be kind to yourself if the inventory reveals areas in which you need to improve. You might be surprised how your relationship with your children improves when you learn and practice the art of validation.

Your children need to sense safety and stability from you. Your home is the secure base from which they operate. For healthy child development at any age, you must provide stability at home. John Bowlby, known as the father of attachment theory, set forth the idea of the parent as a secure base that children could return to after exploring the world. He pointed out that kids need their parents to be dependable, supportive, and safe. When parents fail to provide this for their children, their children develop attachment wounds, and future relationships are likely to suffer as a result of these wounds.[5] As you navigate the difficulties of single parenting, you must check in with yourself to make sure that your own difficulties, the unhealed wounds from your past, are not rendering you unstable for your children.

If you completed the inventory above, and feel good about the way you're parenting, bravo for you! If you find areas that you need to improve upon, seek help and improve. Be gentle with yourself: any pilot knows that a plane is only truly on course 5 percent of the time. The other 95 percent, they are making corrections. Take this to heart and don't beat yourself up if you perceive that you have failed in this area. It is never too late to love your children well!

Why Your Response to Your Children Matters

Depending on their developmental stage, children can be very egocentric. Because of their magical thinking— naturally believing that everything revolves around them— they can internalize self-blame. This blame becomes the enduring story that they continue to tell themselves. They take cues from how parents act and create their story from their experience of us. We, as parents, have a great impact on whether their story is healthy or traumatic. Begin listening to and validating your children today so that their stories will end well.

The next chapter will focus on giving yourself grace if what you have done up to this point isn't your best. When you know better, you do better.

CHAPTER 17

Accepting Imperfection

L ynn shook as she relived the details of her divorce trial.

"I did all of the things I was supposed to do, but the judge still chose to give all of the franchises to Bobby," she moaned. "If I had just told him about all of the ways I was involved, he would have understood that I could have handled it. I know I could've handled it. Don't you think I could've run those businesses?"

I listened as she described how she would see her ex-husband at an upcoming holiday gathering, and how he would likely be with his new girlfriend. "Do you feel ready to handle that?" I probed.

"Yes, I will be just fine," Lynn responded. "I know where to get an amazing outfit, and I have been losing weight!"

In euphoria, Lynn described her latest fashion find as if she were picturing herself strutting down the runway, sporting the latest Yves Saint Laurent hot-pants-and-crop-top duo. "Oh, he will so regret choosing her!" Lynn vowed.

Weeks later, Lynn landed in my office, describing her crash after the event. "I saw them standing in the corner. I had a migraine, but I knew I could push through it. By the time I actually got the chance to say exactly what I had planned to say at the perfect moment, Bobby was interrupted by a phone call and they had to leave in a rush. After that, I went home and violently threw up because of the stress and was in bed for three days with a migraine."

In this scenario, Lynn was blind to her perfectionism and performance-based thinking. She did not see a single way that she could've avoided that situation. Weeks later, when she came in to talk through the fact that she got an invitation to a family wedding and had to take her children, I asked her to describe what she felt in her body. She reported a tight neck, muscle tension in her shoulders, and a flipping stomach. She was beginning to see how her body reacted to thinking about a very stressful future event.

I offered a suggestion. "Do you think you could bow out of this one?"

"Well, no!" she insisted. "I can handle it!"

Yet she began to drift into dreamland again, deciding what was in vogue and how she would look in the new fad. Her mantra was something like, "I can handle anything. If I just look good enough, it will all be okay and people will see how strong I am for my children." And off she went, continuing to ignore her body and continuing to march through the pain.

Accepting Our Limitations

Stephen

Admitting "I just can't handle it!" destroys the myth of perfectionism. Stacey eventually learned this credo as she began to set boundaries with others. But it was a novel concept to a strong woman who prided herself on handling everything.

I can't stress this enough to those I counsel: when we accept our limitations and learn to be honest with ourselves, a great sense of peace and relief will follow. Too often, it takes a hard lesson to get us there. We feel that we are our own worst enemy, and that we have taken on way more than we can handle. As a single parent, we can participate in or cause our own abuse, taking on things that we truly were never designed to handle. We send a message to others that says, "Use me, because I will say yes!"

Why do we behave this way? Because, internally, we don't truly ever feel good enough without performing to make someone happy.

This chapter is going to cut like a machete into those heavily guarded areas where we are vulnerable in our single parenting endeavors. We're sorry, but not sorry, for going here with you. We are sorry because we know that looking into your deepest insecurities is a scary, vulnerable exercise. We are sorry because we know it hurts and that, more than likely, you have subconsciously avoided it for a very long time. Yet we're not sorry, because it is a life-giving message that you need to hear. And we are honored to open—ever so carefully—this Pandora's Box with those who are in desperate need.

So, brace yourself as we gently pull out and process motives for saying "yes" and attempting to do so much. Like most who struggle in this way, you probably learned it as a survival skill growing up. And sometimes, single parenting feels like survival. Questions such as, "Tell me about your parents. What is your birth order number?" help us understand and explain how perfectionism in childhood can create lifelong patterns. If your grades and good behavior give your parents a feeling of pride in their parenting abilities, you will repeat those behaviors. If parents praise good behavior as a distraction from someone else in the family who is messing up, a child feels like he must continue to perform or risk upsetting the apple cart. So, the behavior continues. As an adult, you believe that being perfect is tied to your identity of being a single parent. Your internal belief goes something like this: *I am good if I do it right or well enough, or to please someone else.*

Perfectionism is a role often played by a firstborn. Oldest children frequently become the hero children whose role is to make the family look good by doing everything right. If you are a firstborn or this feels familiar, avoid the temptation to look the other way. Instead, look inward and examine these truths. The good news is that relief and freedom are waiting on the other side of the fear and pain. Once you look past the "musts" or "shoulds," you will find Christ's unconditional love waiting for you, and it is oh so refreshing! He is there, waiting to pick up the slack of the things you can't do by yourself as a single parent.

The most common belief we hear is, "I am not good enough." If you are honest with yourself, you will likely hear those voices in your head. There are so many times in single parenting when you make mistakes and feel like you have damaged your children—times in which you fear judgment that is most likely just your own. In these moments, remember to give yourself grace and turn to God, who amply lavishes mercy and grace on your mistakes. He knows that we will fail.

He is ready to meet our failure with open arms. Maybe, tucked in with your need to be perfect, you have gained a belief about God that says, "I must be perfect to please Him." If this is the case, go back and check your theology, because you've adopted a limiting belief about God that is untrue, according to the Bible. People say, "I know this is not true, but I just can't get it down to my heart."

Stacey uses EMDR to help clients get positive cognitions deep down into their souls. It is a remarkable approach that uses bilateral stimulation of the brain similar to the left-right eye movement that occurs during REM sleep, or tones or taps to receive the same effect. This stimulation works to move a memory that has been incorrectly stored to a more functional part of the brain.

Here's what's going on inside our brains: During stressful or traumatic events, our brains process and store information and memories incorrectly. Often, similar situations reinforce these memories over time. EMDR changes the beliefs to more functional, positive ones. So, thinking *I am not enough* moves to *I am enough*. The belief that *I have to perform to be acceptable* moves to *I am fine as I am*.

Through this practice, the body releases built-up tension, stress, and paralysis. This results in torrents of relief. Here's what we suggest: Seek out a therapist who utilizes this mechanism at www.emdria.org if the elevator of your mind won't descend into your heart.

Our Identity in Christ

Stacey

Along with EMDR, my growth came as I studied the classic Christian book *The Search for Significance*.[1] The pages of that book and workbook became worn and marked up over the years as I led groups to the same freedom that I was finding. I deconstructed the judgmental, harsh God that had evolved and flourished in my head. I began to reconstruct my worth based on the unconditional love of Christ. I applied my new knowledge to my new status as a practitioner in the arena of single parenting. I learned that I was acceptable—even when I punished my kids too hard. I was worthy of love—even when I was rejected by my ex-husband, or my dates, or my kids. I was forgiven—even when I let an off-color word fly in the face of a challenging day. I was complete in Christ—even when the house was a total disaster area. I used to walk around the block in my early days of being separated with a worn copy of the Truth Card Declaration from *The Search for Significance*:

Because of Christ's redemption,
I am a new creation of infinite worth.
I am deeply loved,
I am completely forgiven,
I am fully pleasing to God,
I am totally accepted by God
I am absolutely complete in Christ.
When my performance
reflects my new identity in Christ,
that reflection is dynamically unique.
There has never been another person like me
in the history of mankind,
nor will there ever be,
God has made me an original, one of a kind, a special person.[2]

That ragged little card nestled in my wallet for many years. I would pull it out when I was feeling bad about myself. I then would insert whatever I thought was the worst of the worst behavior behind each phrase, like, "I am deeply loved, even when my kids say they hate me" or "I am completely forgiven when I have thoughts of running away to Tahiti and deserting my kids" or "I am fully pleasing to God, even when

I drank too much wine the night before." I would end with the greatest reminder of all: "I am totally accepted by God, even when I told my child to get out of my face and that I couldn't stand the sight of her."

That tattered tally of truisms walked many a mile with me. In a sense, I was doing EMDR on myself as I pondered the words, coupled with the motion of my feet as I walked. In the process of staying healthy, I was healing my body and my mind at the same time. In fact, walking was how the originator of the theory of EMDR, Francine Shapiro, discovered that bilateral stimulation aided the brain in processing difficult emotions.[3]

The Old Testament is chock-full of rules, commands, and consequences to sin. Today, we don't don our sackcloth or use ashes as makeup to our display our offenses. Why don't we? Because our loving Heavenly Father knew that we could not fulfill all of those requirements, yet He still wanted us in right standing with Him. So, He sent His Son to atone for our sins, so that we could be made righteous with Him (Romans 8:1–4). Why would we strive to be perfect single parents when this amazing gift of freedom has been given to us? He wants to give us a hand along the way. He wants to give weary single parents a rest! (Matthew 11:28–30)

Be Still

Brenda was a highly accomplished engineer client of mine. Trying to get her to be still and quiet her mind was like trying to change a three-ring circus performance into a solitary, high-wire act. Brenda gasped when I suggested that she empty her mind and focus on her breathing. Her backstory: the day she was going to pick up her daughter at the adoption agency, her husband came out as gay. Although she was devastated that her future was in no way going to resemble what she had dreamed, she wisely chose to continue on her mission. Today, she is raising a lively little girl named Lillie while her ex-husband lives with his male lover in a separate home. Brenda has a lot to hold together on most days. To get her information-superhighway-brain to a slow down to a meandering country lane was no easy task.

I remember Brenda telling me after her trip to Colorado, "I finally get it! I have to stay grounded and still myself in the present to be able to keep control of myself and my emotions, and then I can make good decisions about what to do!"

She told me about sitting high atop Pikes Peak and just taking in the view, her breathing slowing as sat in awe of the natural beauty. Brenda realized that it took a vacation in a scenic setting to help her understand the grounding that we had been practicing in my office. After that, she began to sense when she was running too fast or too hard. She knew she needed to stop *doing* and remind herself to just be a human being. I reminded Brenda that my dad used to say, "Stacey, remember to be a human *being*, not a human doing!"

Practical Ways to Integrate New Ideas

Start with copying the Truth Card Declaration and begin reviewing it twice daily. Put a copy on your bathroom mirror, computer monitor, or on the fridge.

In an article about how to stop beating yourself up with perfectionism,[4] therapist Matthew Jones lists nine helpful ways to give yourself a break.

Nine Ways to Accept Your Limitations

1. Tweak and create more realistic goals. Make them shorter-term and easier to accomplish.
2. Dispute your negative self-talk. Give yourself margin for error.
3. Say "no" more often. It is a two-letter word. Just say it!
4. Practice self-care. It is okay to take a break, a nap, or spend money on a massage.

5. Remember that time off is not wasted time. It is time spent on your physical and mental health.
6. Schedule breaks and vacations. These are utterly important to your well-being.
7. Trust God that it will get done. Letting go and surrendering is the essence of faith.
8. Remember that multitasking is not very efficient. Be present with one thing at a time.
9. Reassess and lower your expectations and standards for others. Give them a break as well.

These won't be easy to begin with. Remember, perfectionism is a pattern that you have been practicing over a lifetime. It will take time for your brain to initiate change. Give yourself grace throughout the process. When you begin to let up on all the pressure, you will see relief in your mind, body, soul, and spirit. That relief will spur you on to more changes. Before long, you will be more settled and relaxed.

Drink in the Delight

When you begin slowing down, you will naturally become more present with your children. They will notice it. Really, they will feel it! That is what we all want, to be present with our children and not miss the moments of wonder that organically happen with young ones. There is nothing like watching them experience a peaceful snowfall for the first time, or the exhilarating snowball fight that ensues. Perhaps it's the first time they throw a line in the water and feel that tug on the rod, and the look in their faces of intoxicated anticipation of what could be on the end of that taut string. Maybe it's the joy of a carousel ride or playing in the waves of the ocean. None of these things can be thoroughly enjoyed if a to-do list is taking up space in your brain, especially if a neighboring inventory of "shoulds" and "oughts" jostle for your attention.

Bottom line: Work through your ideals of perfection. Accept your limitations. Embrace the power of the Perfect Father in Heaven. You and God make a complete team, even without another parent. Let Him fill the gaps; let others fill the gaps. Parenting is fraught with mistakes. Accept imperfection and embrace it. It is normal to lose one's temper at times. Recover and apologize.

The focus of this chapter has been on training your mind. If you end up in an alcoholic haze day after day, your identity in Christ doesn't change, but there is a pattern that must be dealt with and changed. Reframing your mind is not an excuse for bad behavior. If you blow it with your kids, recognize it and repent. Then change the behavior. And, for heaven's sake, if you are recognizing the limitation of being able to do it on your own, get help from a professional! The healthiest people I know accept their powerlessness and embrace recovery!

As you begin to accept that you are imperfect, you will begin to thrive. Giving up the strive to thrive actually helps the thriving come to fruition.

CHAPTER 18

You're Doing It!: Thriving as a Parent

You made it after all. You made it another day. And you can make it one more. You're doing just fine.

Charlotte Eriksson

Being single and a parent is not a death sentence. Shifting your perspective can change the course of events in your life. You can go from surviving to thriving. It doesn't need to be a shame-filled experience. Instead, you can be whole and flourish as a person and as a parent, because you have all the necessary ingredients and steps to move forward in a positive direction. The journey ahead can be bright if you take into account all you have learned in the previous chapters. Remember, work through your own baggage, grieve your losses, and stay out of victim mode. Don't forget to recognize your limitations. Create a village and ask for help. Put God in the center of your life and seek Him daily, and His promises will come true for you in your journey. Remember not to let others' perceptions define you. Below are dictionary definitions of the terms "single" and "parent," the terms I have used to describe you in this book.

Single: Only one; not one of several

Parent: A father or mother

The dictionary definition may use the word *only* to describe your status. But the antonym of *only* is *accompanied*. Consider yourself accompanied by many other single parents walking this same tough road. Look to your left and right. See the weary warriors walking the walk daily. Take courage and strength from the heroes in this book. We know them; we know that they would say to you, "I've been there. Keep going. You're doing well. Keep it up. Look how far you've come." You are not alone. We bet you don't have to look far in your city or town to find others like you. If you are all honest with each other, you are in the same boat, paddling up the same stream and having the same difficulties. Reach out and get help. Reach out and be a help to a fellow single parent. Accompany and be accompanied.

Most importantly, you are accompanied by the best Companion we can think of. He is all-powerful and omniscient (better than any spouse around!). He is the Master of the Universe who wants to walk this walk beside you. He will be there when you kick and scream, when you fail, and when you fall. He will keep loving you no matter what you do. Whether you are a single dad or a single mom, God is waiting to romance you. Christ's words in John 3:16–18, quoted below, demonstrate an incredibly deep and amazing love—something our finite minds cannot begin to comprehend. We just have to trust . . . and believe!

> This is how much God loved the world: He gave his Son, His one and only Son. And this is why: so that no one need be destroyed; by believing in Him, anyone can have a whole and lasting life. God didn't go to all the trouble of sending His Son merely to point an accusing finger, telling the world how bad it was. He came to help, to put the world right again. Anyone who trusts in Him is acquitted; anyone who refuses to trust Him has long since been under the death sentence without knowing it. And why? Because of that person's failure to believe in the one-of-a-kind Son of God when introduced to Him. (John 3:16–18, MSG)

We don't know of any fleshly human being who can fill that bill. Welcome Him on this journey with you. Your children will thrive right alongside you and God! Things won't be perfect. Nothing on this earth is meant to be. But everything will be just right. Decide every day to give it your best, using the tools mentioned here. Ask for help and forgive yourself along the way.

We wish we could look each of you straight in the eyes, hug you, and tell you, *"You got this!"* So, go look in the mirror, arms crossed at your chest as if you were giving yourself a hug, and say, *"You got this!"* Now go kick single-parenting tail!

Notes

Chapter 1: You Got This: Parenting Well

1. Andrea Redd, "Raising a Godly Family as a Single Mom," Focus on the Family, 2007, https://www.focusonthefamily.ca /content/raising-a-godly-family-as-a-single-mom.
2. Annamarya Scaccia, "Celebrities Who Were Raised by Single Parents," Simplemost, September 19, 2018, https://www .simplemost.com/celebrities-raised-by-single-parents.
3. Julie Lythcott-Haims, "How to Raise Successful Kids— without Over-Parenting," TED video, 14:07, October 2015, https://www.ted.com/talks/julie_lythcott_haims_how_to_raise _successful_kids_without_over_parenting?language=en.
4. Melinda Ratini, "What Are the Advantages of a Single-Parent Family?" MedicineNet, September 8, 2021, https://www .medicinenet.com/what_are_the_advantages_of_a_single -parent_family/article.htm.

5. Victoria Prooday and Eliza Murphy, "Kids' Work Ethic Is in a Crisis and We, the Parents, Have a Lot to Do with It," Love What Matters, https://www.lovewhatmatters.com/kids-work -ethic-is-in-a-crisis-and-we-the-parents-have-a-lot-to-do-with -it.

6. Ibid.

7. Kelly Musick and Ann Meier, "Are Both Parents Always Better than One? Parental Conflict and Young-Adult Well-Being," *Social Science Research* 39, no. 5 (September 2010): 814–30, https://doi.org/10.1016/j.ssresearch.2010.03.002.

Chapter 2: In the Beginning: Surviving the Early Days

1. Daniel Amen, "The Number One Habit to Develop in Order to Feel More Positive," Amen Clinics, August 16, 2016, https:// www.amenclinics.com/blog/number-one-habit-develop-order-feel-positive/.

Chapter 3: Mask On or Mask Off?: Feeling Your Grief

1. Elisabeth Kübler-Ross, *On Death and Dying* (New York: Collier Books/Macmillan Publishing, 1970), 37–109.

2. Goran Šimić et al., "Understanding Emotions: Origins and Roles of the Amygdala," *Biomolecules* 11, no. 6 (May 2021): 823, https://doi.org/10.3390/biom11060823.

3. Gary Sibcy, "NEUR 103: Applications: Practice Models and Neurobiology," Lecture presented at Light University, November 21, 2016.

4. "Tear Bottle History," Lachrymatory.com, May 22, 2008, http://www.lachrymatory.com/History.htm.
5. Dr. Sheri Keffer, interviewed by Stacey Sadler, November 22, 2020.

Chapter 4: No Surrogates, Please: Letting Your Children Be Children

1. Susan Peabody, "Emotional Incest," The Fix, May 18, 2018, https://www.thefix.com/living-sober/emotional-incest.
2. Ivan Boszormenyi-Nagy, *Invisible Loyalties* (London: Routledge, 2014), 165.

Chapter 5: Put on Your Own Oxygen Mask: Practicing Self-Care

1. Judith Herman, *Trauma and Recovery* (New York: Basic Books, 1997), 160–61.
2. Robert S. McGee, *The Search for Significance: Seeing Your True Worth Through God's Eyes* (Nashville: Thomas Nelson, 2003), 31.

Chapter 6: God Is My Coparent: Receiving God's Guidance

1. *Alcoholics Anonymous: The Story of How More than One Hundred Men Have Recovered from Alcoholism* (New York: Works Publishing/Alcoholics Anonymous World Services, 2014), 59.

Chapter 7: A Faithful Provider: Receiving God's Provision

1. Yuan-Chiao Lu et al., "Inequalities in Poverty and Income between Single Mothers and Fathers," *International Journal of Environmental Research and Public Health* 17, no. 1 (January 2020): 135, https://doi.org/10.3390/ijerph17010135.

2. Alysse ElHage, "Five Facts about Today's Single Fathers," Institute for Family Studies, December 5, 2017, https://ifstudies.org/blog/five-facts-about-todays-single-fathers.

Chapter 8: It Takes a Village: Receiving from Others

1. Bella DePaulo, "It Takes a Single Person to Create a Village," *Psychology Today*, April 21, 2008, https://www.psychologytoday.com/us/blog/living-single/200804/it-takes-single-person-create-village.

2. Matilda Chew, "When It Takes a Village," Centre for Perinatal Health and Parenting, March 26, 2020, https://www.perinatalhealth.com.au/blog/when-it-takes-a-village.

Chapter 9: Misfit: Noticing the Discomfort of Singleness

1. Mike Friedrich, "Census Bureau Releases New Estimates on America's Families and Living Arrangements," United States Census Bureau, December 2, 2020, https://www. census.gov/newsroom/press-releases/2020/estimates-families-living-arrangements.html.

2. Ibid.

3. W. Bradford Wilcox and Hal Boyd, "The Nuclear Family Is Still Indispensable," *Atlantic*, February 21, 2020, https://amp .theatlantic.com/amp/article/606841.

4. "American Culture: Family Structure," Cultural Atlas, 2022, https://culturalatlas.sbs.com.au/american-culture/american -culture-family.

5. Jyn, "7 Comforting Stories of Loneliness in the Bible," Faithful Motherhood, https://faithfulmotherhood.com/loneliness-in-the -bible.

Chapter 10: The Scarlet Letter: Healing from Shame

1. Patrick A. Means, *Men's Secret Wars* (Grand Rapids: Revell, 1999), 225–26.

2. Pat Springle, *Untangling Relationships: A Christian Perspective on Codependency* (Nashville: LifeWay Press, 1995), 30.

3. Brené Brown, "The Power of Vulnerability," TED video, 20:03, June 2010, https://www.ted.com/talks/brene_brown_the _power_of_vulnerability.

Chapter 11: Crippling Thinking: Rejecting Victimhood Mentality

1. Andrea Mathews, "The Victim Identity," *Psychology Today*, February 24, 2011, https://www.psychologytoday.com/us/blog /traversing-the-inner-terrain/201102/the-victim-identity.

2. Erik Erikson, *Identity: Youth and Crisis* (New York: W. W. Norton, 1968), 94.

Chapter 12: Dealing with Your Child's Other Parent: Modeling Health Relationships with Adults

1. Deborah Serani, "The Do's and Don'ts of Co-Parenting Well," *Psychology Today*, March 28, 2012, https://www .psychologytoday.com/us/blog/two-takesdepression/201203/ the-dos-and-donts-coparenting-well.

Chapter 13: When You're the Bad Guy: Setting Boundaries for Your Child

1. Henry Cloud and John Townsend, *Boundaries with Kids Workbook: When to Say Yes, When to Say No, to Help Your Children Gain Control of Their Lives* (Grand Rapids, Michigan: Zondervan, 1998), 65.

Chapter 14: Am I Ready?: Dating as a Single Parent

1. Ron Deal, "11 Best Practices for Dating as a Single Parent," FamilyLife, January 31, 2019, https://www.familylife.com /articles/topics/parenting/parenting-challenges/single-parenting /11-best-practices-for-dating-as-a-single-parent.

2. Margot Starbuck, *The Grown Woman's Guide to Online Dating: Lessons Learned While Swiping Right, Snapping Selfies, and Analyzing Emojis* (Nashville: Thomas Nelson, 2020), 113.

3. David Elkind, "Egocentrism in Adolescence," *Child Development* 38, no. 4 (December 1967): 1025–34, https:// www.jstor.org/stable/1127100?origin=crossref.

4. C. S. Lewis, *The Four Loves* (San Francisco: HarperOne, 2017), 169–70.

Chapter 15: Attitude of Gratitude: Choosing Thankfulness

1. Ann Voskamp, *One Thousand Gifts: A Dare to Live Fully Right Where You Are* (Grand Rapids, Michigan: Zondervan, 2015), 139.
2. Ibid.
3. Madhuleena Roy Chowdhury, "The Neuroscience of Gratitude and How It Affects Anxiety and Grief," Positive Psychology, updated March 25, 2022, https://positivepsychology.com/neuroscience-of-gratitude.
4. Ibid.
5. Michele Borba, "Curbing the Youth Entitlement Epidemic," Michele Borba, Ed.D., August 8, 2009, https://micheleborba.com/building-moral-intelligence-and-character/michele-borba-curbing-the-youth-entitlement-epidemic/.

Chapter 16: Holding Space

1. Taylor Bennett, "What Are Positive Parenting Skills? A Licensed Marriage and Family Therapist Delves into Four Important Skills a Parent Can Offer Their Child," Thriveworks, July 18, 2018, https://thriveworks.com/blog/positive-parenting-skills-parents-offer-child.
2. Ibid.
3. Ibid.

4. Pat Springle, *Untangling Relationships; A Christian Perspective on Codependency* (Merritt Island, FL: Rapha Publishing, 2003), 45–49.
5. John Bowlby, *A Secure Base: Parent-Child Attachment and Healthy Human Development* (London: Basic Books, 1988), 36.

Chapter 17: Accepting Imperfection
1. Robert S. McGee, *The Search for Significance: Seeing Your True Worth Through God's Eyes* (Nashville: Thomas Nelson, 2003), 147–48.
2. Ibid.
3. Francine Shapiro, *Eye Movement Desensitization and Reprocessing (EMDR) Therapy, Third Edition: Basic Principles, Protocols, and Procedures* (New York: The Guilford Press, 2018), 7.
4. Matthew Jones, "Perfectionist? 10 Ways to Stop Being Your Own Worst Enemy," Inc., September 8, 2016, https://www.inc.com/matthew-jones/perfectionist-10-ways-to-stop-being-your-own-worst-enemy.html.